A Christian Woman book
Solo

Elizabeth Flynn was born in London's East End and grew up as the youngest of a large and loving family. She now lives alone in a flat in central London, a lifestyle which she finds equally enjoyable and fulfilling. An actress by profession, she currently spends much of her time writing which she combines with a wide variety of temporary jobs in offices and in the theatre. She firmly believes that living alone gives great opportunities for the deepening of a person's awareness of God as well as for the maturing of their own character. Not only that, it can be great fun.

Christian Woman Books

Series Editor: Gail Lawther

Creativity
Using your talents
Eileen Mitson and others

Family Planning
The ethics and practicalities
of birth control methods
Gail Lawther

Alone with God
Making the most of your
quiet time
Jean Holl

A Woman's Privilege
Jean Brand

Birthright?
A Christian woman
looks at abortion
Maureen Long

Eating for Health
Janet Mutter

Children under
Pressure
Pat Wynnejones

For Better, For Worse?
A realistic view of problems
in Christian marriage
Julie Reeves

Solo

A positive guide to living alone

ELIZABETH FLYNN

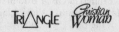

First published 1987
Triangle/SPCK
Holy Trinity Church
Marylebone Road
London NW1 4DU

British Library Cataloguing in Publication Data

Flynn, Elizabeth
    Solo: a positive guide to living alone.
    —— (Christian woman books).
    1. Single people   2. Loneliness ——
    Religious aspects —— Christianity
    I. Title   II. Series
    261.8′3588   BV4596.S5
    ISBN 0–281–04285–3

Phototypeset by Input Typesetting Ltd, London
Printed in Great Britain by
Hazell Watson & Viney Limited
Member of the BPCC group Aylesbury, Bucks

Contents

Acknowledgements

The author gratefully acknowledges the help given towards the production of this book by the following people: Malcolm Douglas, Tony Jasper, Cindy Kent and Pauline Walker.

Series Editor's Foreword

Christian women are developing a new awareness of the way our faith touches every part of our lives. Women who have always lived in a Christian environment are facing up to the important issues in the world around them. Women who have found in Christ a new direction for living are seeking to sort out the problems that are hampering their spiritual growth. And many women are rediscovering the joy in using their God-given talents, in their relationships with God and with other people, and in their spiritual lives and worship. *Christian Woman* magazine has been privileged to be part of this learning process.

As a result of this deepening awareness and commitment to Christianity, many books have been published which help women to sort out what God can do for them as women, as wives, as career people, as mothers, as single women. Most of these books however have been rooted in the American culture; this *Christian Woman* series has come into being because we believe it is important that we have books that talk our own language, and are relevant to everyday life in our own culture.

Each book in this series will deal with some aspect of living as a Christian woman in today's world. I am delighted that we have been able to be part of the blossoming of God's church in this way. We hope that the books will help you as a Christian woman to overcome problems, enrich your life and your relationships, learn more of God, think through important issues, enjoy your femininity, make wise choices, and deepen your commitment to Jesus Christ.

In these books we have invited people to share what they have learned about living as Christians. Not everyone will agree with all the ideas expressed in each book, but I know that you will find every book in the series interesting and thought-provoking.

Books change people's lives – perhaps these books will change your life.

GAIL LAWTHER

1

It's not what you are,
it's the way that you live it

'Oh I couldn't live on my own, I wouldn't be the type.'

A lot of people probably think that's a very reasonable statement. Even if they haven't voiced it themselves they might very well identify with it. But (like thousands of others) I live on my own. So does that make me a special type? I don't think it does. Let me explain.

I grew up in a large family in the East End of London. My twin brother and myself were the babies of six children and for a few years during my childhood my maternal grandmother lived with us. So the house was usually packed to capacity. Once a friend of one of my brothers was reported as saying to his mother in amazement, 'You should see their teapot.' This amused us at the time but the size of our teapot (large by any but NAAFI standards) had never seemed odd to us. I remember I had a friend along the road who was an only child. In her house one day she was telling me the evening seating arrangements for her family.

'That's mum's chair,' she said, pointing to an armchair. 'That's where dad sits (pointing to the other one) and I get the whole of the settee all to myself.' With which remark she stretched out luxuriously on it. In my home at the time, apart from the sacrosanct mum's, dad's and nan's seats you had to get to the living-room early to bag the best places. And if you had to leave your seat during the evening for any reason you could virtually guarantee that your place would have been filled by the time you came back and you would be relegated to a hard seat or the floor. But for all that, when my friend the only child was telling me about

1

'her' sofa, all I could think was that she must have been very lonely. I couldn't imagine living in a home where you didn't have to take a headcount just to make sure that everyone was there. I didn't think very differently for many years, until one day I took a boyfriend home for a coffee prior to going somewhere else. The family had extended somewhat by this time, but even accounting for a sister-in-law or two (my siblings are all male) there were probably less than half of them present on this occasion.

As we were driving away my boyfriend said, 'You know, I don't think I could stand the density of population in your house for more than half a day.' Since I had been regretting the fact that the house had seemed rather empty so that he didn't get the chance to meet more of the mob I was somewhat taken aback by his remarks. Until then I'd never realised that a person might not be happiest when surrounded by lots of people.

Growing up in a situation something akin to the main concourse at Waterloo Station might not seem like a good training (no pun intended) for living alone; but as all men are created equal they are also created adaptable. By the time I came to move into my own place I was not only ready but eager for a bit of peace and quiet. And if there's one thing that growing up in a large family gives you it's a true sense of the value of privacy.

This potted and much-peopled autobiography might seem a strange way to begin a book about living alone; but it's not really. People who live alone have all sorts of histories, all sorts of reasons for their solitary state and all sorts of ways of adapting to their different circumstances.

We are, in fact, all types.

One man's meat

We meet all kinds of reactions from those around us who are ensconced, happily or otherwise, with spouses, flatmates or families. 'Don't you get lonely?' is one that I get now and again, or, more subjectively, 'I would be frightened all on my own.'

I suppose, in general, there are two main groups of people who are on their own. Those who haven't chosen it and who would prefer to be sharing their home and/or life, and those who have chosen it and wouldn't swap if they did get the chance. With these two outlooks of course you get a 'never-the-twain' kind of situation. Each group cannot possibly understand the other point of view. An acquaintance of mine was once called upon to give a talk on her life-style. (She lives on her own and revels in it.) Up she got and dived into an enthusiastic dissertation on how wonderful the single and solo life is. She thought she had done a good job (the business of making the speech had been rather sprung on her at the last moment). However, once she had sat down, feeling rather satisfied with her effort, there came a comment from the floor.

'It's all right for you,' said a disgruntled voice, 'you chose to live like that.'

And therein lies the rub.

It's not much fun being on your own when you don't want to be. My acquaintance went away thinking that she had, after all, been rather selfish and unthinking in her approach.

If you are living alone and hating every moment of it you have my deepest sympathy. But the only comfort I can offer you is that I hope this book will be of some help. Because, as you've probably already realised, like it or loathe it, the fact remains that you *are* on your own and surely it behoves you as a Christian to accept that state as being God's will for you for however long he chooses. If you are expending a great deal of time and energy thinking about what life *could* be like or how you'd like things to be, then you are not getting on with the job of serving the Lord in the way that things *are*. Not only does this not serve God, it doesn't serve the Christian community nor the world at large and it certainly doesn't help you.

As I mentioned earlier . . .

. . . There are all sorts of different reasons for being alone and whatever your one is will colour your life-style. A single woman either without family or at a great distance from them will have to go out and find her company. She will have to build up relationships at her church, place of work and any club or social organisation to which she belongs. It is then up to her to open her home to those she wishes to invite for a meal, a coffee or whatever . . . For a woman living within easy reach of her relatives the situation will probably be different. This can be a two-edged sword. You might love spending time with various members of your family and, in return, receiving visits from them. But in some cases it doesn't work out like that. I have a friend who is, to all intents and purposes, leading an independent life in a flat but seems to be forever at the beck and call of her family to help this member with some job or that one with the loan of some money. I feel sorry for her sometimes when she tells me of some of the running around she is expected to do. Running around, incidentally, for which I feel sure she wouldn't be called upon if she was married. Some people don't seem to realise that Aunt Jane has her own life to lead and might not welcome the opportunity to come round whenever the occasion presents itself to sit with someone or to be permanently available for babysitting.

Then there are the widowed, separated and divorced, all of whom, apart from their own families, might very well be retaining ties with their late or ex-husband's relatives. Also, in the case of the divorced and separated, their ex-husbands could quite possibly be 'on the scene' in one capacity or another. For all of these people there is the possibility of being descended on, with or without prior warning, by an assortment of relatives or offspring.

Yet again there are those who, through no fault of their own or otherwise, live as though in an ivory tower, neither visiting nor receiving visits. It's impossible to gauge how many live like that in our society.

So for some people, living alone might mean not seeing anybody but the milkman or the postman from one month to the next. While for others it might mean that they hardly ever seem to get a moment of their waking hours to themselves. And all that still doesn't allow for the fact that in cases of the widowed and single there might be a man friend in the picture. I suppose all this is leading up to one thing. Being alone doesn't necessarily mean being lonely. Because let's face it, if you're miserable in your solitariness, it's probably not because you're alone but because you're lonely.

The other person's grass

You have probably come across the old saw about how you can be lonely even in the middle of a crowd. It's trotted out so often that it's almost a cliché; but it's nonetheless true for all that. If you are really unhappy in your state just think. Surely it can't be more miserable than having to endure a deeply unhappy marriage – now there's a loneliness none of us would relish. Or what about a more simple situation such as, say, living with people who are just 'not your type'. I know some might be inclined to put up with such a life on the grounds that any company is better than no company at all; but really, is that the right answer? I don't think so.

Whilst I've said that my background may not have been a good training for living alone I think the opposite is also true. Living alone is certainly no preparation for sharing your life. We who live alone have to answer to no one. We eat when we are hungry, we come and go as we please. We watch what we want to watch on the television and generally, if we're fed up with the world we simply shut our door on it. It's a tremendous freedom but you have to be careful not to let yourself become isolated (more of that later).

For those living alone life has probably the same balance

of advantages and disadvantages as it has for anybody in any other situation. And, as with a lot of things, it's what you make of it. You can submit to it and find peace or fight against it and waste a lot of energy. It can give you great opportunities for spiritual growth and a maturing of your own personality. Although it might seem like a contradiction in terms you can find yourself becoming more outgoing and open as a person. You can grow closer to God and deepen your prayer life to a depth and degree of understanding you might otherwise not have reached.

Conversely, you can become bitter and twisted and withdrawn.

It all depends, as with everything else, on your response to God's call to you as an individual.

While I was writing this book, I talked to several other people, men as well as women, who live alone, and asked them to share their own experiences and points of view about the solo life. I have interspersed their 'Personal Views' among my own chapters.

Roger Royle

Roger Royle, the son of a clergyman, was born in Cardiff in 1939. He studied both at university and theological college and is an ordained priest in the Church of England. Among the posts he has held have been Succentor of Southwark Cathedral and Senior Chaplain at Eton College. He is now an honorary curate and earns his living as a writer and broadcaster, contributing regularly to a weekly woman's magazine and to the BBC.

I've lived alone now for eighteen years, and it is something I'm used to. It was not always the case. I once lived as a curate in a clergy house. I had to share then; and obviously, living in colleges you've got to live in community.

I think in some ways, with the type of life that I lead now, it is just as well that I *do* live on my own, because I'm often under such pressure that it would be very difficult for anyone else to cope with me. I'm an honorary curate of a parish and I earn my living entirely as a writer and a broadcaster. I'm not married – and people who are not married tend, on the whole, to live on their own. It isn't as though I have a huge house and therefore would want others to fill the house with me. I'm in a small flat which is very convenient for one person, and that's how I exist.

I have learned how to cook and how to look after myself, and how to be a host to other people; because I think that if you live on your own (or even if you don't) you ought always to make your home available to other people.

In some ways there is an extra financial pressure if one lives on one's own, because there is no one to share the household expenditure. But in other ways you can regulate it – for instance, if you are worried about heating bills, you can always move into one room and keep that warm and huddle in it, whereas if you have a family you've got a responsibility to make sure there is more warmth throughout the house. This greater flexibility with your own money ought to make you more responsible, but there can be a tendency too, if you are not careful, for it to make you more selfish and just pander to your own needs.

I don't think living alone has in any way affected my spiritual life. There is no reason why living with somebody or not should have anything to do with it at all. But I have noticed that those who have got someone to share with are more conscientious about the smaller sides to spirituality, like saying grace before a meal. When there are two or more of you having a meal together you will probably say a prayer as a thank-you at the start. Whereas, if you're on your own, you are more likely sitting on a stool by the sink grabbing something and it doesn't cross your mind so much that this would be the correct way to begin. Obviously, too, you miss out on family prayers or shared Bible study. In this respect, I think it is important for a single person to be part of a Christian 'family' in some way or another. I'm looking at the moment at the possibility of having a support prayer group, because my work is very demanding, and takes me all over the place. Someone who lives on his or her own needs to get together with like-minded people (though not too like-minded because you need people to question you) to share problems and thoughts.

One of the things that I enjoy, and I think this is part of my spiritual life, is having ones and twos and threes to a meal in my flat. I don't enjoy giving big parties because I have enough of those. I am not short of meeting crowds of people, but I am short of meeting people as individuals. It is very important that the single person living alone is able to meet with other individuals rather than getting lost in a crowd. It's a hackneyed thing, but you can be just as lonely in a crowd as when you are one your own.

There's a big difference between being lonely and living alone. Yes, there are times in my life when I am very lonely.

But this is true also of the person who is living with other people. In fact, sometimes you can feel more at peace when you're on your own, because you have only got yourself to cope with.

I can understand that a person might dread living on their own if they have just gone through a divorce or a bereavement. Not only are they having to adjust to a totally different way of life, there is also the grief at the loss of their partner. But for a young person growing up, I think it is very wise eventually to move out of the parental home and set up on their own.

It didn't take me long to adapt as a young man. In fact I was rather thrilled about it, because for the first time ever I had somewhere where I could entertain other people. It also meant that I had a home on which I could stamp my personality. Rather than just having one room as a study/bed-sit, I could make sure that people realised that this, for instance, was how I liked my sitting room. Although obviously in those days I couldn't afford the most glamorous of things, I felt that my home reflected my personality, and that was a huge boost.

The only real shock I had as regards living on my own was when I moved from being senior chaplain at Eton College. There I had actually had a house of my own which had five bedrooms and two bathrooms; it was very splendid indeed. My front door was always unlocked and people used to come in and out. During the day it would be boys. In the evenings, other members of the staff would pop in for a drink or a chat, and I enjoyed this very much. The most difficult thing to come to terms with when I moved to London to live in a bed-sit in Brixton, was the fact that I hadn't got that social aspect any longer. I found I had to make an effort to go out to see people and to invite them to my home, whereas for the previous eight years it had been a very natural thing. Making that effort is vital. However tired you feel, or fed up, you have just got to take positive action, otherwise you will be left in the place on your own.

I don't know that I would resent it if I had to share again, because I have always been very grateful for the way in which other people have accepted me into their homes. One of the things I've learned from Australians is their tremendous hospitality. But I do have to work at odd hours, and if someone is staying with me, for instance, it's not like a person keeping normal office hours. My routine is all over the place. For instance, I left home this morning very early but I was back in my flat by half past three and I'm out again this evening. And my dining room is also my spare bedroom because there is a put-u-up sofa in there. So suddenly I find my dining room goes and I have to adjust to that sort of thing. The longest I have had someone to stay is three weeks, and even that put quite a strain on my pattern of life.

I don't fear growing old alone, partly because I think we are a more humane community these days and there are old people's homes and sheltered housing and shared housing. I can see myself fitting in, in some way, to that kind of thing. What I would loathe is to lose a sense of independence and being able to cope. But then, that could happen to anyone.

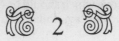

Us and them

There is a well known song which declares that people who need people are the luckiest people. You've probably heard it and although Christians would, I expect, prefer to use the word 'blessed' instead of 'lucky' there's a great deal of truth in it. We do need people. We all need relationships. 'Ah, here comes the nitty-gritty,' you might be forgiven for thinking, 'She's going to get down to the business of romance.' I'm reminded here of when I was at my senior school and we arrived in the syllabus at the stage where we had to embark on the study of that nudge-nudge, wink-wink section known as 'human biology'. Full of glee we sat down for the first lesson, waiting for all to be revealed, only to discover that we were expected to copy from our books a picture of the reproductive organs of a frog.

I suppose this section might seem a bit like that. But this book is about living alone so I can't really tell you how to find your man and stop living alone. That's not to say I don't think romantic relationships aren't important or worthwhile – quite the reverse in fact. But let us consider . . . How often have you heard the phrase 'I'd like to have a good relationship' (or words to that effect) on the lips of someone who gets on fine with her family, has lots of friends and fits in well at her place of work. Well, there you are! She has a good relationship, lots of them in fact.

So what really happens is that our hope, wishing or even obsessive longing for that special partner can spoil or dim our appreciation and enjoyment of all the other relationships with which we are blessed. Especially in the case of that very special Love which should be first, last and always in our lives (or yesterday, today and tomorrow, if you prefer).

However, let's get back to my original comment; we all need relationships.

Those who live alone will probably find that they have much more control over and freedom in their relationships than those who don't. At first glance that might seem like an odd statement to make, but just think about it for a moment. If you don't feel like going to the Bible study/cinema/visit/shopping trip with Jane/Fred/Mrs Bloggs, then you simply don't have to. Now I'm not advocating that you let people down on a mere whim but it's much more difficult to avoid these things if you are Jane's flatmate, Fred's wife or Mrs Bloggs' daughter. As I said in chapter 1, if you're fed up with the world you simply shut your door on it. And though it doesn't do to shut your door on it too much, because it will tend to forget you exist, it's here, actually speaking, that living alone can be of some help to you.

Queen in your castle

You have the right to choose who comes into your home and who doesn't. You can have one friend in for a meal or the whole gang over for coffee. It's entirely up to you – or is it? Opinions sometimes differ on this score. I'll tell you what I mean. I once had to go into the country with two friends for a weekend conference. We stayed at a charming cottage owned by a friend of one of our party.

'It's very nice of you to put up with the three of us,' I said to our hostess at some point over the weekend.

'Oh that's all right,' she replied cheerfully, 'I don't think that my home ought to be mine exclusively, I think it ought to be made available for other people.'

Now to some people that might sound a bit drastic. But to others it might sound like no more nor less than what must be expected from any Christian, living alone or otherwise. On the other end of the scale I'm sure I've been used in the past by this person or that to stay in my flat for a night or two because I've been a bit of an easy touch. So my first stop in this look at relationships with the world around us is this sticky issue.

Right, you're the mistress of this home. God has given you this place and put you in the position of authority in it. Be confident of that authority. It's as well to be aware that in living alone you might be more vulnerable than others to requests from your minister, for instance, to put up a visiting speaker; or from a friend wanting to stop over because it's convenient for some reason or another. That's great, or it could be. The speaker might be a refreshing and interesting guest and the friend someone you haven't seen for a while and with whom you're longing to catch up on all the news. Beware though of the time your heart sinks instead of jumps, because you've been asked 'yet again' to receive a visitor or because a chum rings and asks you if you're in next Saturday and you immediately know that she's not going to suggest a night out with you but the use of your spare bed after a night out with someone else. Even this last one is all right now and again but if you start to feel suspicious that you are being used don't feel guilty about it. Look at your suspicions, examine them and don't be frightened to say enough is enough. Even if you use more diplomatic language than that (and you probably will) the point is the same. If you feel that you're in the right, be firm. Remember, you have the authority.

I'm not saying that you should only have guests when you feel like it. There are times when we all have to do something we don't particularly want to do and we should accept it in a Christian spirit. But it's your home, not a hotel. Never be afraid to consider the means of the person who wants to stay. They might well be able to afford a bed-and-breakfast place. Without being rude you can explain that you can't put them up for that night but that you are happy to book them into a nearby economical hotel. Only you know how to handle the situation you might find yourself in. It might seem a very difficult thing for you because you feel as though you're being rude by refusing. But others aren't always so sensitive.

This could even apply to someone at your church who might make you feel guilty (or try to) because you don't want to play the hostess again. However you do it, once you've made up your mind, stick to it. Remember, it's tiring to have people to stay, even when they're welcome. I've been in this situation once or twice. It's not much fun, there's no easy way to handle it and perhaps you might find yourself risking a friendship that had formerly been of value and comfort to you. But then, if it *is* a worthwhile friendship nothing should be lost; after all, we should be able to be truly honest with our genuine friends. Let's face it, you're not talking about turning away people that are really stuck. It's just that, as you should consider the needs of others, so should they also consider yours.

I suppose the same can be said when it's just a case of people who, though welcome, pop in just a little more often than you'd like for a cup of tea and a chat. People can wear out their welcome in this way as in any other, and it's better not to let it get to the pitch where bad feeling is likely to be caused. People aren't generally offended by a smiling 'I'm sorry, do you mind if I turn you out now? I've got a job to do/bath to take/need an early night.' Different generations are obviously going to use different phraseologies, but if people realise that you intend to be alone when you want to be then they will also realise that when you say, 'Do come round this evening,' their company is genuinely desired and valued.

Of course things aren't always cut and dried. I think that's a good thing, and when life is flexible you should be prepared to get flexible with it. It can be very comforting to hear, 'Yoo hoo, it's only me,' coming from the front door, and surprise visits, like surprise invitations, can be great fun.

Right, so that's you established as queen in your domain. What about you when you're out visiting? Let's face it, we are probably all guilty of getting on someone's nerves at one time or another or of wearing out our welcome somewhere. It's probably a necessary part of the growing and learning process, and if you can say to yourself, 'No I don't think I'd better visit Jean tonight,' or, 'I can see Mary wants to be alone so I'll go,' then you've either got or are on the way to getting the balance right.

But if you are one of the unhappy people who haven't chosen their solitary lifestyle then you might find yourself in danger of becoming something of an offender here. Some people just can't bear their own company, they can't stay in their own homes alone. . . . So they spend a lot of time in other people's.

A couple of years ago a friend and I spent a few days visiting another friend who lives in a coastal area. Whilst there, our host and hostess threw a dinner party. It was an extremely pleasant evening and at about midnight, amidst 'goodbyes' and 'see you in church tomorrows', the bunch left. We thought everybody had gone but came back into the dining room to find a lone guest still there.

'Oh I thought you'd gone as well Terri,' said my hostess (her name wasn't Terri of course).

'Oh I'm not going yet,' was the reply. Well, we chatted on for a while longer until our host and hostess eventually said that they were going to bed. Terri then left (in a huff, I later discovered). It was by now about one o'clock.

After church next morning our hostess fell into conversation with another couple from the parish.

'I heard you had Terri round last night,' said the wife.

'Oh yes,' said my hostess, 'how did you know?'

'She came round to us afterwards.'

Yes, that is what I'm saying. Terri had turned up on this other couple's doorstep at gone one in the morning.

'Oh my goodness, that's a bit much!' you might think. And you would be right. And you wouldn't go that far. But then, Terri, in all probability, didn't think she was going too far. She just needed company. Actually speaking in this case, as far as I could gather in my short visit, Terri was tolerated fairly well. But it's a salutory lesson to remember. If you live alone and you hate to be alone you are going to need all your friends. So it's as well not to turn them into enemies. Do you really want to have your company only tolerated when it could be welcomed? In fact, are you clinging to your friends because you are desperate for them? You know, that's giving them rather a burden to carry.

Mind you, I'd like to make it clear that I'm not referring here to those times, such as bereavement or some other sort of sorrow, when we might feel the need to be with people a great deal more than usual. All the same, while we are on the subject of the intrusive behaviour of your friends and relatives or of your intrusive behaviour to them, let's take a quick look (and it need only be a quick look) at the intrusiveness of those people we should never welcome.

Not wanted on board

Living alone can make you more vulnerable to suspicious callers, both on foot and by telephone. If you haven't already done so, put a chain on your front door or a spyhole, both if you can. Never feel silly to call out 'Who's there?' before opening your door to a knock or ring of the bell. Even if a strange voice calls out that they're from a cleaning company or something of that nature there's still no need to open the door. 'No thank you, I don't need any cleaning done/the hedge cut/the dog walked,' can be heard clearly through the wood. The simple rule is, if you're at all suspicious, don't open the door. And even if you do, make sure you keep the chain on.

Dealing with obscene phone calls is even easier. Simply hang up. If you are getting a lot of them, or one persistent caller, you can arrange for British Telecom to have your incoming calls monitored, or even for your number to be changed. If you manage to work out roughly when the calls are likely to occur (even perverts have to have some sort of routine) perhaps you can arrange for a male relative or friend to answer the telephone for you. It might just frighten the caller off or at least make him think the game isn't worth the candle. Whatever you do don't worry about it. Obscene phone calls are rarely personal (whatever they sound like) and if you ask around at your church or place of work you will probably find that virtually everybody has a dirty phone call story to tell.

It would be as well to mention here also that it's probably not a good idea to answer your telephone with your number. If you're in the habit of picking up the instrument and saying, 'Hello, Anywhereville 1213?,' try and get into the way of just saying the first word of that greeting. You might think it sounds abrupt at first, or even rude, but honestly it doesn't. And don't be intimidated by the caller. If he/she says, 'Hello, what number is that please?' reply, politely but firmly, 'what number did you want?' A genuine caller will respect your reserve.

Eight hours a day

If you sit down and analyse it you will find that you've got several relationships operating on various different levels.

Apart from friends, family and the people at your church there are those with whom you work. Working relationships always used to puzzle me. I suppose this was because I spent so much time flitting from one office to another as a temp. Some places were a hotbed of bitchiness and gossip while in others everybody seemed too busy to talk much. Yet again in others, the atmosphere was friendly. Whatever the situation is like at your place of work though, you have to spend approximately eight hours out of every twenty-four there, so really, the more harmonious it is, the better.

Sometimes, genuine, out-of-office friendships can arise from your working situation and sometimes you put your colleagues out of your mind at the end of the day along with the work. Every situation is different and the only real test of any friendship begun in the office (or wherever you work) is how it develops and grows outside of working hours.

And relationships, to be of value of course, have to develop and grow.

This is where Christians will find themselves taking into account matters that the rest of the world might not think to consider. In fact, for Christians, this *is* where I get to the nitty-gritty! The one relationship in our lives which should guard, guide and give life to all the others is our relationship with God.

As you grow in the Lord you will find that your friend-ships, especially your closest ones, are with your fellow Christians. This is only natural. After all, the herding instinct is as strong among us as it is in any other group of people. But there's another reason. There's an awful lot that you can't easily confide or share with your non-Christian colleagues and friends. The best intentioned of them will listen politely, will feel glad for you when you're glad and will probably try to understand. And they will certainly try to accept your different view of life. But in the long run, unless they are converted, much as they might like you, you will be the person who is dubbed 'rather religious'. Of course this is not a hard and fast rule and you might find you get on like a house on fire with your friend who is agnostic/atheist (or even from a completely different religion) whilst you are often at odds with Christians of your acquaintance. However, I think it's generally true to say that a relationship, particularly a close one, has to be nourished. And one of the things that will feed it is being able to share with the other person everything that's important to you. And not just sharing in the sense of your being able to talk about your prayer needs or what lessons you think the Lord is teaching you at that moment; but to receive the same sort of confidences back in return. Christian conversation, while not constantly 'holy', will necessarily contain unembarrassed and matter-of-fact references to our spiritual lives. No matter how sympathetic they may be, the agnostic (etcetera) will not fully understand this extra dimension. Remember, we have 'life in abundance', a gift which doesn't even begin to be explained by the words 'rather religious'. So you will probably find, as time goes on, that there are gaps in your conversations with your non-Christian friends, things you don't say. And not being fully able to talk about the most important thing in your life is not conducive to a thriving, growing relationship of any sort.

All this is not to say that you should avoid relationships with non-Christians (what sort of witness would that be?). It's just that, by the nature of things, such friendships will be limited.

What has this last section got to do with living alone? you might ask. Okay, fair question; it's just that, if you are living alone you are going to be more dependent on *all* your relationships than if you weren't. They are going to loom larger than they would otherwise and play a more important role. In fact, that brings me back to where I began this chapter – 'people who need people'. Living alone will give you much more opportunity for becoming a hermit, but much less excuse.

That's all very well, you might be thinking. All that talk about inviting people round or going to visit them. But what if you don't know anybody? What if you don't feel in tune with the people at your church (or it's just not that social) and you work in an office by yourself?

Yes, well all that could apply . . . which leads on to chapter 3.

Nadia Thompson

Nadia Thompson, now in her late thirties, was born in Cairo of an Egyptian mother and an English father. She works in London as a television researcher for the Canadian Broadcasting Corporation. She is also a member of an interdenominational Christian community.

I suppose I live alone first of all through personal circumstances – I'm not married and most people my age are. (Though I suppose that's a sweeping statement to make in inner London, because here I guess the proportion of single people must be going up all the time.) I also live on my own by choice. I could have shared a flat, but the chance came for me to have my own place, which was a great thing and I really enjoy it.

For me, the experience of living alone was interrupted by a period of sharing when I came to London seven years ago and, in a way, I would say that the sharing has changed me. As a student, many years ago, I had lived in a house shared by ten people, with a different record playing on every floor – it was all great fun. After that, living on my own, in one room first of all, then a larger place, was part of growing up; and coming back to sharing was also a formative thing. And now it has changed me to live alone again – because people keep changing all their lives if they are open to the Lord. All circumstances change you, and if you don't change you should start worrying.

I've learned lessons at every stage of change. Having to share taught me something about myself after years of being alone. You learn a lot by being rubbed against other people – about your bad habits, petty irritations and so on. Living with someone shows you what still needs to be dealt with in your life as a Christian. It certainly did with me. And it's been a blessing for me in a way being given the time and the opportunity since to work at these things on my own. I've learned to do that. I have had a chance to meditate, I suppose, on what happened when I was sharing, and to confront myself in a more spiritual way in my prayer time – because you get more chance of doing that when you're on your own. You can pray when you like, get up when you like, come in when you like. Which is not the case when you live with other people and you're confronted with other people's tastes and other people's timings.

You meet with the Lord more often, living alone, because your need is greater – especially as a woman, I think. If you haven't got a husband or confidante to turn to, to sit down with and have a good session getting things off your chest about what annoyed you today or what really excited you or worried you, then you have to turn to the Lord. And for me, it's made me look to him more, instead of to other people, for my emotional needs; and it's made me expect him to answer me more than I did before. It's also made me appreciate myself. I can see my own value, perhaps, living on my own, because I can live in relation to the Lord, and I take my identity from him rather than from another person. This gives me confidence. My self-image has increased since living alone, through knowing I can do it, me and the Lord – we're a great team! I'm very happy at the moment.

Living on your own has a lot of practical advantages – like being able to cook what you want, or not having to say when you're going to be in for the benefit of the other cook or cooks. And then there is the silence when you come in. At first, being on my own again for the first time after the happy bedlam of sharing, I found it a bit sad. Now I find it enriching. Especially coming in after a day at the office in the centre of London and commuting – the thoughts that fill your head are not exactly Christian when you're standing on the tube through twelve or thirteen stops. Then you come home and there's this enriching silence.

I don't get recurring comments about my lifestyle – perhaps because I don't meet so many different people asking me personal questions. I suppose if my colleagues at work thought of asking me about myself more than they do – you know how it is in an office, you all think you know everybody else so there's not very much personal contact really – I guess if they did examine the situation there would be questions, because most of my colleages are either married or living with somebody of the opposite sex.

I suppose I'd say loneliness is the state of being alone and not wanting to be; suffering from being alone. Which of course you can experience even in a crowd (and I'm sure a lot of people do) and even in a marriage. I can't say that I'm lonely. I'm a Christian and therefore I'm not allowed to be lonely. People of the world in my situation might be, I guess, because they wouldn't have the companionship of the Lord Jesus which the Christian has, or should have. Also, I'm blessed by belonging to a community, a situation which is quite unusual. Even people who belong to a church and who are active in a parish can experience loneliness. But I have people living near me who belong to my Christian group which is inter-denominational; so near that I can be in eight or nine of their houses within five minutes' walk. That is a real privilege. My brother and his wife (who is one of the people I used to share with) are just five minutes' walk away too. I suppose I'm in a situation more usual in a village or small provincial town, of having very good friends who are also committed to my Christian way of life and who also live very near, near enough for them to be of help and a day-to-day support in every sense, spiritual and practical.

I don't fear growing old alone for the same reasons. I've got my family for a start (I mean my blood relations), though it is small. And my extended family, that is to say, the Christian family. It's a very big part, and a permanent part, of my life. We've made commitments to each other. We've actually signed on the dotted line, so to speak. Although a lot of us have come to London from different parts of the

22

world, as well as of the country, we've decided to stay here, against all odds. If the community were moved to, for instance, Milton Keynes, I would move to Milton Keynes.

If anyone asked my advice about living alone I would say, don't be afraid of it. Find yourself fellowship first of all. I'm taking into account that you have the Lord in your life in a real way, and that he's not a relative stranger whom you have to discover. Because if you have to cultivate him as well as other people you've got a lot of work to do. Concentrate on the relationships that you have with other Christians. Don't worry too much if you don't have everybody at work falling all over you and inviting you round, or if they never come to see you. Make your Christian relationships the priority, because they're the ones that are eventually going to feed you, even though they might seem unpromising or unlikely at the start – because you don't really know the area, or for whatever reason. The Lord will provide. He knows what you need; somebody will pop up. And if you're faithful to him, he will honour that faithfulness.

It didn't really take me long to adapt to living alone, partly because, as I said, I belong to a Christian community. There are people who live alone and who consequently shut themselves up. Partly it's because they're tired – I mean, who isn't after a day at work? They go home and switch on Wogan or whatever it is and sit in front of the television. Whereas all my life, even before I became a Christian, when I've lived alone I've tended to go out to people, and I've been fortunate perhaps in having the personality to do that. I've probably become less extrovert in my older years because I've liked my own company more than I did then, but I still tend to go out and visit people. As I said, it's been made very easy.

I would share again if the Lord wanted me to. He'd help me through any irritations. I think I'd be more open to him now, having learned what I have from my previous experience. I could approach the thing more correctly perhaps than if I had never shared before. I think there are definitely parts of me that are being cossetted at the moment through living alone. I would have a rude awakening if I shared again with somebody, but it probably would be quite good for me. But if it wasn't of the Lord, or if I wasn't a hundred per cent sure, I probably wouldn't do it. I feel I'd say no. I wouldn't have anybody foisted on me; I wouldn't be put upon. I think this is something that's quite important to point out to people who are on their own – because you're a Christian you don't have to say yes to everything! If you're not absolutely sure, don't do it; that's my advice.

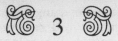

3

You're not alone, alone

I would like to begin this chapter by saying that living alone can be tremendous fun, and then go on at great and enthusiastic length about the sheer pleasure of being able to shut your door on the outside world and slopping around in your old clothes (or no clothes) without having to account to anybody for anything.

However, not everyone's like me. When Mary, one of my sisters-in-law, was single, she shared a flat with another girl. Whenever Mary wasn't in, this flatmate, not being able to stand being on her own in the place, went out as well. You might be more like that, in which case you are probably not happy with your lot. Or it may be that you are shortly having to face the prospect of living alone for one reason or another and are dreading it.

Well, you'll soon discover, though you may not believe it at the moment, that you'll get used to it. Millions have before you. However, whether you grow accustomed to it as a cross to be born or because you discover it's an unexpected and delightful blessing is something that only you can explore.

I've entitled this chapter, 'You're not alone, alone', and I mean it. In fact you're in plentiful company. Which observation won't be of much help to you if you're stuck within the four walls of your home and you feel like crawling up them just to make a change from watching the wallpaper fade. I'm not planning to take an in-depth look at loneliness here. I don't think there's any real point. If you're going, or have been, through it then there's probably nothing I can tell you. Furthermore, my task in this book is to encourage an optimistic and positive approach. So my attitude here must be, not, 'What is loneliness?' but, 'What can be done about it?'

Now I don't know why you're lonely, how deep your loneliness goes or how it affects you. But I do know one thing. Nobody is going to beat a path to your door. That is, they won't unless they know you're there. And even if they know you're there, they've still got to know that they will receive a welcome. All of which is saying one thing. Whether you turn people away or draw them towards you; it's within you. Within your attitude and response to those around you – which I suppose makes me break my own rule about looking at the question of loneliness. But in trying to deal with the problem you must first discover why you've got it.

New girl in town

Yes, quite an obvious one this. If, for any reason, you move a considerable distance from home you will discover in a new kind of way what communities are all about, how they work and the kind of support they can be to their members. You will realise all this because you are now no longer a part of one.

You will also see how so many of your relationships came about simply because you were a member of that community from which you came. Your best friend was someone in your class at school or a member of the same Guide company; and you met your first boyfriend at the school dance or church youth group. In fact, your entire circle was made up from people living in that community. In a way, they were given to you on a plate. This doesn't make them any less valuable or God-given. But it does mean that now you're away from them you're going to have to make more of an effort. And let's face it, effort is something none of us like to make.

A few years ago I was living in a bed-sit in south London. It was the usual sort of situation, a large house with each

26

room made into a bed-sit and the other residents and myself rarely seeing each other except when coming, going or passing on the stairs. I remember in particular one quiet Sunday (a very quiet Sunday) there came a knock at my door and I opened it to find the girl from the next room standing on the landing. She wondered, she said, if I wasn't doing anything that afternoon, would I like to go to the common with her as there was some sort of town show on. I thanked her and said yes I would, and we had a pleasant afternoon together. From that we got to know each other better so that it was no longer just a passing-on-the-stairs relationship.

Now you might shudder at the thought of tapping on someone's door and I wouldn't blame you. I don't know that I could either and I think it was very brave of my bed-sit neighbour to break the ice. But I have never forgotten or ceased to feel grateful to that girl for making the first move. And even though at the time I wasn't particularly lonely it taught me a valuable lesson.

The reasons most people wouldn't feel able to knock on their neighbour's door are shyness, fear of rebuff, looking small and silly, and because in doing so they're making a public announcement of the fact that they haven't got anybody in particular as a friend and therefore might appear to be inadequate in some way. In fact, they're all reasons to do with ego.

Since there are all sorts of devotional aids/treatises/ sermons and Christian literature on the subject of ego versus Christ, I'm not going to go into it from that point of view. What I will say is this. My erstwhile neighbour, when she knocked on my door that Sunday, didn't look in the least small, silly, friendliness or inadequate. She looked like a pleasant young woman from next door being neighbourly. For all I know she might have formed the impression that it was me who needed a friend (as I recall, I was a bit of a hermit at the time). And as for the fear of rebuffal. Well, who would? Why should you be rebuffed? A person would have to be pretty mean to waste energy by being so unkind. Think of it logically; would you react like that if your neighbour knocked on your door and offered you a gesture of friendship?

However, if you're still shuddering don't worry. You don't have to go knocking on people's doors. But suppose there's someone you see regularly. Do you look at the ground when you pass them as so many of us do? Do you study your feet whilst waiting in the queue at the bus stop with the same people who wait there every morning? I'm not suggesting you imitate the Cheshire Cat or anything like that, but a smile won't go amiss; perhaps you can throw in a cheery 'good-morning' as a bonus. If the other person doesn't respond don't be put off. It might only be because of shock and they'll grin back the next day having had twenty-four hours to get used to the idea. And anyway, what if they don't? It's their loss, not yours, if they can't even return a civil greeting.

All this isn't necessarily going to get you invited anywhere or give you a deep and meaningful relationship (although you never know). But you will find yourself becoming more and more confident as you learn that each effort isn't really so frightening and that you don't get looked at as though you're mad.

Probably you will have already got involved with a church nearby and, if you haven't made any friends there yet, just remember that the same rules apply. If, as I mentioned in the last chapter, it doesn't have much in the way of social activities, why not find another church in the area which offers more? This doesn't have to mean that you're changing your allegiance (for those committed to a particular denomination) but it will broaden your outlook.

Above all, be patient. All the relationships you had at home took a long time to develop; it's just that you probably didn't notice this because you were growing up with them. Well it's the same here. Things don't happen overnight.

Last one in

It might seem a bit like that at times – the only person left in what might once have been a thriving and jolly circle. One of your friends might have moved to another area (please refer them to the previous section!). Another may have got married and now, naturally enough, will have less time to spare. Another could have emigrated and perhaps you felt that another one and yourself were never particularly compatible so would not even be able to maintain a conversation, let alone a relationship.

So suddenly you feel you have few or no friends you can call upon. I think it must happen to all of us at some time or another, and really there's no need to worry about it. If you had enough friends who you were compatible with and you mutually enjoyed time spent together, the chances are that you are outgoing and friendly enough and will soon find other people to fill the gaps. Nothing is static in this life, and if you stay alert and prayerful you will be able to take the changes in your social circle with a sense of peace and even eager anticipation at what might happen next. And anyway, just because you don't see a person so often it doesn't mean that you lose their friendship, just that the nature of relationship must necessarily change. And you've got to be prepared to change with it.

My best friend

Best friends are terrific. I've got one and her friendship is a tremendous source of comfort to me. We pray for each other; we have a giggle together and we share confidences. We are not, however, joined at the hip. She has other friends and so have I. We are not dependent on each other for our entire social lives and we do not live in each other's pockets.

You've got to be careful not to be too dependent on one person. It can be very draining, especially if, as can happen, one of you is rather retiring and finds it difficult to socialise.

Then the stronger, more outgoing person finds herself carrying her companion to some extent. Not only can this become exhausting, it can sound the death knell of the whole relationship more surely than anything else. The stronger character, even if she doesn't want to, might very well find her affection for her friend turning to dislike simply because of the burdens being placed upon her within the relationship.

If you're the sort of person who finds it very difficult to make friends and therefore have very few, you might have to be strict with yourself to make sure that, in your need for your friends, you don't actually push them away from you. If you find it happening to you, it might be a help to bring it into the open. Show that you're aware of the problem. You could very well find that your best friend is only too happy to help you to mix more with other people.

The frightened mouse

And if you are a very shy person you are in a particularly sad sort of situation. Praying about it is, naturally, your first recourse. But asking the Lord for confidence doesn't mean that you'll be able to breeze into the next vicarage party with a 'hello everyone' which arrests the entire gathering as you walk through the door. There are, however, a few tricks you can adopt which should at least help you to find your feet in a crowd.

The first and perhaps the most useful one is that, if you keel over and die inside at the very thought of speaking to anyone, just remember, you don't have to (talk to anyone that is). Good listeners are always, but always, in demand. Everybody has something they want to say and if they can find a willing audience they will take on the burden of the conversation for you. (As an interesting by-line, it's amazing how much you learn about people simply by listening to them.) Gradually you will grow in confidence and feel able to contribute.

It's as well to bear in mind also that if you are a shy person you might well be the only one who's aware of it. People who are shy, because of that very fact, can often come across as rude and uncommunicative. Try to get a picture of what you appear like to others. Imagine you are looking at yourself over the shoulder of someone who is talking to you so that you can get an idea of how you might come across. I remember once feeling quite hurt at a party when I addressed an innocent and friendly remark to one of the other guests whom I knew vaguely. I forget what the question was and it's not important now anyway but his answer, in the affirmative, was a very short 'yes'. He didn't even look in my direction once and his whole attitude discouraged further comment. Feeling that I had been snubbed I mentioned it to someone else later. 'Oh yes,' I was told, 'that's because he's very shy.' And looking back, I can now see times when I might have appeared rude to people because, in my turn, I was rather shy at the time.

Join the party

I speak figuratively of course. In the previous chapter I mentioned the herding instinct. It's very true. My eldest brother, as a much younger man, was very keen on anything to do with motor-cycles and racing them. Before too long it seemed that most of his friends were of a like mind, and they filled the house with their great leather boots and riding suits and drank gallons of my mum's tea out of cups held in their oily hands and talked piston rings, brake cables and cubic capacity. My twin, Edward, and myself were thrilled when we were given a gentle spin round the block perched up on the petrol tank. Later, when we were bigger, we were able to ride on the pillion and, quite frankly, it still rates as one of my favourite forms of travel. Another brother, I remember, had a great interest in fishing. He joined a local angling club and I got used to not opening any strange tins that I found around the place just in case a horde of maggots tried to escape.

These are just two examples. Birds of a feather flock

together. Most people have something in their lives which gives them a great deal of recreational pleasure. And, unless your hobby is stamp-collecting, reading or listening to records (complete with earphones on), then there is bound to be some organisation or evening classes in your area where you can meet others who share the same interests. You might think that you're not the 'clubby' type and I can well understand that feeling. But on the other hand if you really have a very meagre circle of friends, then by getting out to something like that you will at least have made a start, made an effort. And as we all know, big trees from little acorns grow. You can find out about most of the social clubs and organisations in your area from the local library, town hall, or even the local paper.

If there's something particular you want to do, I would suggest you do it even though it might involve joining a secular organisation. It's not a good idea, unless you are feeling rather vulnerable in your faith, to wrap yourself up in 'spiritual cotton wool'. We have to mix with all sorts in this world and even though the people at the local amateur dramatic society might not have any particular beliefs the chances are that they will be well disposed and unlikely to threaten yours in any way. On this subject, it's a good thing to mix with non-Christians. You take Christ with you wherever you go and you don't need me to tell you how important it is for them to meet him.

And don't be frightened, unless your conscience leads you against it, to go into the pub with the others for a drink after a keep-fit class or a strenuous game of tennis. You don't have to drink alcohol if you don't want to. My personal feeling is that a moderate social drinker is a better witness than someone who never touches the stuff on the grounds that it is evil.

Having said all that, at the end of the day Christians are naturally interested in the things of God. We want to be able to discuss the Gospel, to join together in worship and generally to know that those around us are similarly inclined.

So for any Christian, especially those living alone (or with non-Christians), the first port of call will probably be their church.

Churches differ vastly in the spiritual and social activities they provide, and only you are in a position to find out what's going on at the one you go to. If, however, your church doesn't have very much in the way of prayer/study/ discussion groups and very little in the purely social line, there's nothing to stop you asking the minister/priest/vicar if you can initiate something. You never know, the poor overworked clergyman might be glad of some assistance in the parish. Here again, don't let the fact that you might be shy or scared put you off. Initially it will probably only mean either a word with your minister or a notice in the church newsletter inquiring if anyone is interested in a 'coffee and chat' session once a week, or a Bible study. It doesn't even necessarily have to be anything spiritual. You could suggest a rambling club, a theatre outing group – in fact an 'anything' meeting. You never know what you might be starting, but you've got to cast your bread upon the waters before you can find out.

It's as well to remember here that there are many people living alone who, for reasons of age and incapacity, can't get out much and are desperate for company. Your church might run a group that visits the housebound. If they don't and you feel led to this sort of action but don't feel you can start such a group, there's bound to be a secular organisation of that nature in your area.

Enforced idleness

Yes, it's no fun being unemployed. This is where one of the major disadvantages of living alone comes to light. Your long, lonely day is not even relieved by the prospect of husband/flatmate/other members of the family coming home in the evening.

I'm not about to repeat everything I've already said about loneliness but I would strongly advise you, if you are in this situation, not to fall into the very tempting trap of lying in bed until late in the morning because you have nothing to get up for. I know from personal experience how easily this can set the pattern of your day – sluggish. Once you're up and ready to face the world half the morning or more could be gone and strangely enough, instead of being able to think 'well at least that's most of another dreary morning done with' you will find that your depression has deepened, not lightened.

Apart from your quest for work you will be wise to find some sort of activity to fill your days. This might seem easier said than done, but the Christian can often find herself in an advantageous position here. You already have contacts; there are people at your church. There are probably daytime activities to become involved with. Have lunch with your friends now and again. Even if it means travelling to their place of work and fighting down your feelings of envy that they have only an hour to spare while you've got the whole day to kill. Try not to think like that in any case (if you have been); the Lord's time is meant to be used, not killed. You aren't sentenced to spending long hours reading the newspapers in the local library, walking (slowly) round the park or making a lunchtime drink in the local pub stretch from opening to closing time because it's preferable to going back to an empty flat. Even so, the library, the park and the pub aren't the pits (well, yes, I know some pubs are). Do try and get out for some part of each day, and even if you don't talk to anyone the fact that there are people around will cheer you up. I know that being cheered up at this stage in your life might only be the difference between being miserable and being very miserable, but given the choice . . . Also, in getting out, you'll at least be getting away from the routine (and monotony) of what might seem, at the time, like a boring, dead-end and very depressing existence. Remember, God is leading you through this time of trial and your task is to keep close to him so that you may learn what his purpose is for you.

Above all, your time of being unemployed can be a time of great spiritual renewal. You now have time for prayer and contemplation such as you don't normally get unless you're on some kind of retreat. I don't mean you've got to join your hands, close your eyes and pray for a set time each day (though of course if that works for you and him . . .). But if you are the type of person who likes to have the radio or records or the television going when in the house try to get into the habit of turning them off, even if only for a short time each day. Learn to enjoy the silence. You can think in the silence; you can contemplate; you can pray, even when you're about some household task. But most of all, you can listen.

Tony Jasper

Tony Jasper is a writer, broadcaster, journalist and Methodist lay preacher. He is the author of fifty books, among them being Cliff *(the approved story of Cliff Richard) and* Jesus in a Pop Culture. *In more recent years he has also turned to dramatic writing with his libretto*, Religion Can Damage Your Sense of Humour, *and his revue*, Day in the Life.

I live alone by choice . . . and have done all along the line, actually, apart from the first few years after university when I lived in a house with open doors. I had my own room, but people wandered to and fro and we shared a common bathroom. But outside of that, I think the reason was, initially, not that I was against living with people; it was because wherever I went people wanted me to fit in with their system – which meant a rota as to who went to the supermarket, a rota for getting breakfast, a rota for washing up. These were much more communal houses, and because of the sort of work which I wanted to do, which was irregular in its hours, I didn't want to be tied down.

When I do mix with people, they tell me I'm a bit selfish. It's not intentional. But I guess when you are with other people, suddenly you have a great problem because you're not used to waiting your turn. You do things when you want to do them, at your own particular time, and like anybody else who does certain things you get into that sort of routine. When I go to conferences and things like that I just muck in and I quite like it for a short period of time. But that is different. I've always considered I can adapt myself to any situation, temporarily.

Living alone wasn't at first a conscious choice, but it's become much more so these days simply because of what I do. Once you've got a little empire – masses of books and records – it's not easily put into somebody's shared flat.

I do feel lonely sometimes. I go away to a conference on a Friday and Saturday and I get back to London about eight o'clock like I did the other day, and I get out of the tube station and the bus queue is full of couples holding hands. And in this particular instance, I remember, there were two groups of people who had invitations to dinner or parties and who asked me where the address was – and in fact I showed one of them the way. You've encountered these happy people, then you go into the empty flat and you've forgotten there's no milk and there's nothing in the freezer . . . and the video's jammed up from the night before and you'd recorded a programme that you'd wanted to watch . . . and because there's nobody there then you feel lonely. But it passes.

I can cope with myself quite well. I rather enjoy, if I get in a certain kind of mood, just wandering round. Or just reading, or sitting in a train. Some years ago I wanted to prove to myself that I could actually be alone all by myself. I drove across America. I think you have to withdraw, and put yourself in a sort of situation to test yourself, which means you can't easily run for security. In other words, you're not within train distance or a bus distance from somebody you know.

I often find I feel rejected when people don't like the things I do. Generally the thing I hate most in this country is that people don't actually say anything about anything. They don't reply to your questions and long silences ensue. This is the British way of doing things rather than saying outright, 'I don't like your radio voice, I don't like your radio programmes'; 'I don't like what you write'. It would be nice to have a shoulder to cry on occasionally, or just somebody to say, 'You are marvellous'. You may not be, but some human being who tells you you're marvellous would make up for this total lack of response that you're getting from the world you work in.

Somebody said to me, and I think it's probably true, that if you don't throw yourself sexually into the normal conventional channels of a relationship with somebody, it goes into your work, into your time. You're much more emotionally involved with what you do. And maybe you lack perspective as well, because you're very close to something and it's very precious to you.

Some married friends of mine told me a couple of years ago (and I've been trying to stop myself doing this – in their company at least), 'Sometimes when we're with you, all you do is talk about yourself.' And my reply to that was, 'Well, you live with your husband and, assuming you have a good relationship, both of you talk about yourselves to each other. And the reason why I talk about myself to you is simply because I've not talked about myself to anybody.' People say, of course, that you should not talk about yourself. That's nonsense, because most human beings talk about their day, even if it's only to gripe about the boss or their manager or whatever.

As for being alone giving me more time for spiritual contemplation – I think I have a basic weakness (it's much easier to talk about weaknesses): I ought to spend more time on it, and I don't. I haven't found, and don't belong to, what I would call a really lively group of people, with whom I can find spiritual comfort, or solace or inspiration. I travel around the country doing a lot of preaching and I'm often away from my local situation. Yet, paradoxically, at the same time I haven't really wanted to be involved on a more practical basis locally, simply because I find that people think that if you write and if you broadcast and you were trained as a teacher as well and you've mixed a bit in drama and things . . . then you're the perfect answer to about nine departments in the church. If you do anything properly, you've got to give a lot of time to it, and if you do the kind of work which I do you find yourself unsure what you're going to be doing next Thursday or Friday.

If you are single, you've got to put up with slight innuendos occasionally from people who think you're gay. It comes up in small ways sometimes. I experienced it the other day from somebody whose son wanted to come to my flat because he knows I've got a big record collection and wanted to hear some records. That was fine with me. Then a little bit later his father phoned up and just the way he used his voice: 'Could he come with a friend?' Maybe I was specially conscious of it at that particular time, but I sensed the boy's parents were a bit uncertain . . . single man in a flat, older man, and perhaps who knows, he might be . . . no real reason to think so but he could be, I mean, after all he *is* single.

There's always a problem that because people in our society tend to think that you're only really normal if you're married to somebody, then maybe you *ought* to be married to somebody. It's a strange world, because if you did marry and divorce they'd be on top of you like a ton of bricks. On the other hand, if you're not . . . I went to my cousin's wedding at which a prominent Evangelical minister gave the address. And I said to my cousins afterwards, 'It wasn't particularly biblical was it.' They were horrified; it had all been to do with the New Testament emphasis on marriage. But I had thought, well, there's a lot of single people wandering around the New Testament too and lots of statements by Paul which people like to avoid, about sex and marriage and women.

I think the hardest thing – and it's got to be remembered all the time – is that if you're a Christian your commitment is to Jesus; but too often you get preoccupied with what people think, what organisations say, what somebody else thinks you ought to be, how you ought to behave. And people put pressure on you to act in a certain kind of way. It's the hardest thing in the world, to be *natural*. I think that's common to anybody – maybe it's more difficult if you're on your own, simply because it's just you and that battle to be yourself.

4

What, not married yet!

An enormous number of people living alone will be single. For women there used to be an unspoken sort of shame that was tied up with the idea that you had never managed to 'catch' a man. For men it was the other way about. They had been clever enough to 'escape' marriage.

Happily however, these ridiculous notions are being eroded away. This is especially so in the case of women who nowadays are able to have more independence in our society that at any other time. I can remember when a woman couldn't get a mortgage on her own or sign a hire-purchase agreement without a man to sign on the vital dotted line. It wasn't so very long ago, and in view of the fact that the ability to earn money and manage accounts is manifestly not gender-linked in any way it was grossly unfair. And thankfully, the days are long gone when a woman had to marry in order to gain 'security'.

So with the change of times comes the changing of attitudes. Nowadays a bachelor might be the first to admit, 'Well, actually I would like to meet a nice girl and settle down'. And equally, a single woman will increasingly not be looked down on by her married sisters as having failed in some way to 'hook' a husband.

But we still meet pockets of resistance. Which brings me back to this chapter heading. More than once have I been greeted at a party or gathering by someone I haven't seen for some years with the words, 'What, not married yet, Elizabeth?'

You've got to be careful how you deal with this one. I

once vowed (a vow I broke naturally) that I wouldn't go to any more family gatherings because I got so fed up with cousin this or uncle that coming up and asking me when I was going to get married.

It's a very boring question. But if you – irritated by being asked it, yet again – give a testy answer (not unnatural under the circumstances), it could be put down in the interpretation of the listeners as frustration (never far from people's minds when it comes to single women). Nor do you want to say 'NO!' aggressively (implying, 'No thank you very much and I don't want to); you might be classed as someone with a grudge against men. There's only one way to deal with the question really. A plain 'no', spoken pleasantly and in the same tone as the question should do it. You don't have to elaborate; you owe nobody any explanations.

But making it clear that you are quite happy living on your own and being able to deal with the enquiries is only part of the problem.

The bulk of it lies in you.

My relations have now given up asking me when I'm going to get married. But at the time that they did, even though I got annoyed with them I was every bit as guilty of the same fault as they were. I too used to ask old friends and acquaintances if they were married or getting married; and I can remember that it was always one of the first things I wondered about any new person I met.

So before we have the right to make any comment about the attitude of those around us to the single state, we really ought to examine our own attitude.

For a start, let's not kid ourselves that marriage isn't important (should you be an offender here). Personally I have a tremendous respect for the sacrament of marriage – it's one of the reasons I'm single. Marriage is very important. All of us came into this world as a result of the mating of a male and a female. For most of us it was within a loving, committed relationship and, genetic engineering notwithstanding, it's going to go on like that until the last days. This is part of God's plan for mankind, and I don't suppose there are many of us who haven't grown up expecting at some time to meet a partner, marry and produce children.

There's no other way of looking at it. The world is a sexual world. It's in the plants, it's in the animals and it's in us. God obviously meant things to be that way and put the seal on the whole business when he made it clear that he came as the Bridegroom for his Bride – us. (The marriage aspect between God and his people was continued from the Old Testament when God took the unfaithful Israelites to task and asked them where was their bill of divorce.)

This doesn't mean that we singles are weird or failing to live according to God's Law. It does mean however, that we have to seek to be at peace with our situation and not to be troubled when we are asked when we're going to get married. The questioner isn't being unreasonable, only human.

The best solution is to show, in the quality of your life, that you are happy and fulfilled. That you are not frustrated or bitter and you are not looking for a possible mate round every corner. People soon learn. And eventually they stop asking you.

Your best friend gets married

Yes, this can be a tricky one. For a start, no matter how easily you make friends there is going to be, initially, a gap in your social life to which you must adapt. More than this though, despite the best will in the world, you might find yourself having to deal with pangs of envy. This needn't be envy in a particular sense; after all, your friend's husband could very well be the type of man you wouldn't touch with a barge-pole even if he were the last man on earth. But envy on a general level is just as much of a temptation. 'Why not me?' 'Why should she have all the luck . . .?' It's a very easy path to find yourself being led along.

If you feel that way, then admit it, to yourself at least.

Pretending it's not there is no way to go about getting rid of the problem. But allowing such feelings and the thoughts they give rise to to gain ascendency will only make you feel worse. And it certainly won't change the situation. You deal with temptation here in the same way that you deal with any other temptation. By prayer, studying the Word of God, reception of the sacraments, staying close to the Lord and, where possible and if necessary, the seeking out of sound Christian companionship and counsel. There's nothing you can do about it after all. Your best friend is going to get married and in her happiness she will want those around her to be glad also. Just because God is giving her what you, in your heart of hearts would like for yourself it doesn't mean you have been forgotten by him. You are still as cherished as ever, still receiving the daily bread that he knows will nourish you best.

So go along and support your friend with a smile on your face and a generous spirit in your heart. It might be your turn next. On the other hand it might never be your turn. Only God knows, and it behoves the Christian to trust that he is doing what is best for us in our lives.

No man is safe

We could easily be back to the barge-pole situation here. There might not be one man among the husbands of your friends who you would look at twice. That won't stop the wives regarding you, even if only in a tiny way, as a threat.

I'm not saying that this is so with most of the married women among your friends or social circle. Quite possibly it won't be and you might be surprised that I've brought it up. However, it *can* occur, and when it does it is probably more indicative of a problem in that particular wife (and/or husband) than you.

You still need to be sensitive though. It's a good idea, if you have to see the husband for any reason, and if it's possible, to make sure the wife is included. Perhaps he is coming round out of kindness to do some job in your home.

Why not ask the wife round as well? You and she can have a chat and a cup of tea whilst he is busy.

But, apart from being sensitive and praying about the confidence and vulnerability of the couple involved, there's not a great deal you can do. After all, you can hardly hang a sign round your neck stating that you don't flirt with married men. As with the question of your singleness, people will just have to learn – in this case, to learn that you're no threat.

Since you've got nothing else to do

This can turn out to be quite an insidious one. On the face of it it's quite natural for people to think that a woman living on her own has more time on her hands than anyone else might have. And perhaps you would find it very nice to be asked to take on this job or that within the church or organisation to which you belong.

But this doesn't mean that you have to be lumbered with every task from changing the water in the church flowers to running the youth club coffee bar. Sometimes it's wise to draw your line and refuse to cross it.

Yes, once again the solution lies in you. Any of us, even women living on our own, can only do so much and people should realise that your time is as precious as if you had a husband and a horde of children to look after. Taking on too much, or letting people persuade you into too many jobs will not only make you tired but will cause you to grow angry and resentful. And try not to fall victim to a misplaced sense of guilt here. This can come about when it seems that there's simply no one else available but you to do a particular job. If you really feel you have enough to do, and especially° if you feel you're not led to that particular task anyway, then be firm . . . and don't budge. Don't be afraid to let people realise that you are prepared for a job to be left undone rather than take yet another burden onto your shoulders. Remember, it's not for others to presume to know what your priorities are, much less dictate what they ought to be.

And when and if you ever get caught in this position don't sidestep or make excuses. Here is a very good piece of advice which I learnt from a cousin of mine.

This particular cousin used to be a teacher in America. Before she had been long in her career she came up against that famous aspect of the American way of life – the Parent/Teacher Association. Now, as a parent she had hated this organisation and as a teacher her views didn't change, so she was never prepared to support them in any way. She found herself under pressure however and it went something like this:

'Are you coming to the meeting tomorrow night, Mavis?'

'Er . . . I don't think I can.'

'Oh, why not?'

'Er . . . (thinking furiously) . . . oh, I have to pick up my youngest from junior high school.'

'Surely your neighbour can collect him. I know Mrs Smith won't mind.'

'Ah yes, but . . . er . . . (panic struck) . . . Bill's parents may be dropping by for dinner later.'

'Oh, but they won't mind you coming away early, will they? And it's only for an hour or so . . .'

Does all that sound familiar to you, in essence at least, if not in detail? My cousin very soon learnt to rewrite the entire script from the beginning. Then it read more like this:

'Are you coming to the meeting tomorrow night, Mavis?'

'No.'

'Er . . . oh . . . er . . . okay then.'

They stopped asking her in the end knowing that if she wanted to do something she would volunteer for it anyway.

But the moral of the story is clear. There is always some thick-skinned or determined person who can tread very firmly on every excuse you can make and squash it flat. So don't give them the opportunity.

Be every bit as active in your church as you feel the Lord is leading you to be. But, single or not, you're not the only one in the community and, if you feel you're being asked to do too much, don't be afraid to put your foot down with a firm hand!

Good old Aunt Jane

It's the same story here really. Only you can show your family that you're not there to be fallen back on every time somebody is needed for baby-sitting/granny-sitting/dog-walking. I'm not anti-family in any way; I love my funny old mob very much. And I'm certainly not against being involved with your relatives and helping them out. But some people get very put upon by their nearest and dearest. Perhaps, to a greater or lesser degree, we're all guilty of it at some time or another and quite probably it's reciprocal. But if you've got the sort of relations who think you've got nothing better to do than sit around waiting for them to call upon you for something, then you'll have to show them that they have another thought coming. You'll just have to try and make sure you have a few prior engagements lined up for when they ring. To coin a phrase, and I don't mean this in an unchristian way, 'You have your own life to lead.'

Theresa Sallnow

Theresa Sallnow was born in Cardiff in 1954. She gained a Master's degree in Theology and then trained as a teacher. She now lectures in Theology and Religion at St Mary's College, Twickenham.

I chose to live alone. I have occasionally shared, as a student, but I never felt cut out for doing so on a general, communal basis. I've always been used to my own company, and found that I was able to pursue different interests alone. I enjoy the company of other people and I like having friends round for meals and generally spending time with them, but it's always nice to know that you can close the door and retreat into yourself.

I have been through phases over the years when I've been less comfortable with my own company. But during the last three or four years I've actually become more content with it. I think you work through the questions like, Should you be living with other people? Should you be married? Should you be this that and the other? and discover that whatever your state of life, and whatever you feel comfortable with, is the right thing for you.

As a teenager I loved being on my own. I was very heavily into solitude. But when I got into my twenties it became a bit more difficult to be alone, I suppose because psychologically I was being conditioned to socialising. But . . . it's a daily adaptation really. It's not something that you say: 'Right, I am now happy to be alone and that's the way it is for all time.' It's a sort of process.

I've learned that one of the dangers of being alone is that you can become very introspective; self-analysis becomes a major occupation, or preoccupation. Too much of that is very unhealthy. A positive discovery is that there are various

47

solitary interests that can be pursued, so that you don't constantly have to be in social situations in order to gain a sense of satisfaction.

As for my spiritual life, for me spiritual life is life experienced as it is. It is day-to-day living, and the spiritual dimension is *that* lived in depth, rather than something added to it. I would see it as important, for anyone living alone, to try to become the full human being that you are called to be, through whatever channels present themselves – whether it be your own particular pursuit of hobbies or making the most of enjoying people when you are with them. And in that sense, spiritually, it's a good discipline.

I do get questions. The most usual one is, 'Don't you get lonely?' And the answer to that is, of course, 'Yes, I do.' But everybody does. The fact of living alone or living with thirty people doesn't do away with the experience of loneliness. It just depends how you handle it. And another question is, 'Why aren't you married?' and then, 'If you're not married then what's wrong with you?' And that again, for me, is from choice at the present time.

When people ask, 'Why aren't you married?' my initial reaction is to say, 'Well, why should I be?' What is particularly important about marriage over against other states of life? But in general I just say, 'At the moment I feel that I have come to enjoy friendships much more, especially in recent years.

Friendships with people of both sexes become more and more important for the single person. If you opt for one special person, you have to be very well aware of the implications of that for all your other friendships, and there has to be a very strong understanding that you don't simply exclude other friends, say, of the opposite sex or whatever, because you've committed yourself to one person. And at the moment I feel I haven't reached the point of being able to work that one out in a satisfactory way which would make it the obvious decision. I don't believe in the head-over-heels business and technicolour sunsets. I think it's a lot more practical than that.

I think loneliness is an awareness of not being complete – that's how it is for me anyway; I suppose everyone experiences it differently. Then the temptation is for your next thought to be, It's because I'm not married, or I haven't got a man, or I'm this, or that, or the other. We are conditioned to believe that, in order to feel complete you have to have another half. But I think for me it's more a sense of there being a degree to which, no matter what, we're always going to feel that, within marriage or outside of it, loneliness is really a part of the human condition, and correctives to it can be found through friendships, through marriage, through solitariness. And my experience of God is very much in and through all that. I'm trying to think of it in terms of a kind of theology; from a Christian perspective loneliness is very much something that is intrinsic to the Christian experience of life. Christ himself knew what loneliness was. And in order to be fully human perhaps this is something we have to experience and live with and live through.

I am afraid of growing old alone. I see my nieces and nephews growing up and I think, Goodness how time passes! And I often find myself thinking that they will be saying to each other, 'It's your turn to have Auntie Theresa here for Christmas this year,' and I think, Do I want to inflict myself in my old age on my family like that? I feel that it's important to try to hang on to an awareness that age is relative, that you are as old as you feel and it's all to do with an attitude to life. But to say that the fear of growing old alone is not there wouldn't be true. It is there and I do feel it. I think it's a fear of growing into a kind of forgotten phase. Because when you're young and you're mobile and you can maintain independence, economically and in every respect, you feel that life is very much ahead of you. But age is something that one has to come to terms with. It's not just the business of becoming physically aged but the passage of time. But I think that that happens anyway; I feel it even now. I look back on the last ten years and I think, What are the next ten going to be like? So it's always a kind of looking back and a looking forward.

One of the first things I would recommend to someone having to live alone is to develop solitary interests. Like some of the things I do: I write and I paint and I listen to music a fair bit as well as reading. It's important to have the kind of things that you feel at peace with doing. Because for people who, maybe, move into an alone situation, the temptation might be to rush out at every available opportunity and find someone to be with, or to spend hours on the telephone. And that's not adapting to the situation. I believe it is important to be with people, reasonably, and enjoy being with people; but that it's actually counter-productive to spend hours with others when you've chosen to live alone. So the development of interests that you actually enjoy on your own is important.

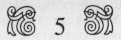

5

You lack nothing

That's right. If you live close to the Lord and are following his commands for you then you are receiving your daily bread in full measure. However, this won't stop you feeling, now and again, as though you are having to make do without your basic rights. In an age of 'rights' it's a terribly easy thing to think that way. We have human rights, voters' rights, consumers' rights, squatters' rights and even animal rights. But when you come to analyse all these rights they amount simply to the (highly laudable) requirement that every one of us treats our fellow creatures with dignity, fairness and consideration. But we don't actually have a 'right' to marriage and motherhood. I want to look at two things in this chapter; the issue of the person who has never been married and that of those who, through separation, divorce or widowhood, are having to face life alone for the first time.

What you've never had you've never missed
That is a curious expression, because even though there's a great deal of truth in it, if you want something very badly you will pine for it and yearn for it and the question of whether this particular desire has ever been fulfilled or not in your past will not even enter into the matter. At the other end of the scale an awful lot of people would agree with the famous adage that it is better to have loved and lost than never to have loved at all.

The real fact of the matter is that if you are without something in your life which you really wish you had, then the pain of not having that thing will be great and hard to bear and neither the wisdom nor the good sense contained in these old sayings will comfort you whatsoever.

For most single women the most obvious lack in their life will be that of a man. This doesn't apply to everyone of course. You may be perfectly happy as you are. However a great many women alone aren't so content, and are missing that special relationship terribly.

Or it may be that you want to have children. You may be in your middle to late thirties and fear that time is running out for you. It can be hard to live with the fact that God has given you so much desire for a child, the certainty in your mind that you have lots of love to give a baby and all the physical facilities necessary for producing one and yet he still denies you. In view of the rising number of horrific stories of child abuse, perpetrated by people who, it seems, don't deserve what they've got, this might be a hard one to take. This problem is not, of course, confined to single women; many married couples are unable to have children.

It is important to remember here that God denies us nothing. And I think it pointless to speculate on why a well adjusted loving woman has neither man nor child while others have both and can't seem to cope with either.

Christians must beware here. We are not immune from becoming bitter and twisted. It's too easy to fall into the trap of closing your heart to God. You can find yourself becoming used to the sadness, seeming emptiness and, ultimately, loneliness, without even realising that this is what's happening. You might even be tempted to wallow in it, as some people 'enjoy ill health'. Be careful of this. Clinging to the darkness can never be God's way. Before you know where you are you will have ended up as the archetypal 'spiteful old spinster' – never an attractive figure.

However, though it's very easy to say, this can be very hard to do, and the only solution is to open yourself to God's healing touch. Even though it might seem at first like a terrifying leap in the dark, he will assuredly lead you into the light, into a fuller life than you would have dreamed possible.

God would not lead you anywhere else.

So whatever your desire is, whatever anguish is burning away in you, there's only one thing to do with it. You must, as always, take it to Jesus Christ. You can offer it up to him in prayer, in reception of the sacraments, in contemplation of his Word and in the comfort of those around you.

By offering it to God you can become transformed. By keeping it to yourself you can become *de*formed.

Remember, no pain, no sadness – like no dark night – lasts forever.

Listening to your friends' stories and seeking a clue to your own solutions will probably not be of much help. There's '. . . I was getting more and more desperate, and when I was about as low as I could get, I suddenly met Jim . . .' And then there's, '. . . I was so desperate, I really thought I couldn't take any more. Then I woke up one morning and I no longer cared; it no longer mattered. Funnily enough, it was shortly after that that I met Fred and, would you believe it, I wasn't interested at first.'

So, from the sublime to the ridiculous and all points in between, every person has a different story to tell.

Of course, as a young woman these questions will probably not loom as large in your mind. You will still be thinking that at some point you will meet a partner and produce children. It's only as the years pass and no one appears on the scene (or even the horizon) that your thoughts will turn to the possibility that you might have to learn to do without.

This isn't the end of the world, though it might seem like it at times. One day you might find yourself glad to escape the tense atmosphere in a friend's house because she and her husband have just had a row or are going through a sticky patch. Or another friend confides to you that she has reached the end of her tether because her children are driving her up the wall and she feels trapped within her house. Then you will remember that there are pros and cons to every situation and, strange though it may seem, those with spouses and children have their moments when they are tempted to look at your life-style with envy.

For the Christian it all comes back to the same thing; and you will find yourself always ending up back here drawing the same conclusion. Our task is to know the Lord, to love and to serve him. And to trust him wherever he may be taking you. One thing is sure. If he wants you to be married then he will bring you to a partner. If he wants you to have children, then children will be given to you, either through birth or adoption.

So you lack nothing. If you have no husband or children it is because you are not meant to have them, not because you lack them. In fact there are no gaps in your life, only fullness of God's blessing. And if you allow yourself to become negative on this issue you will simply be wasting energy.

Mind you, it isn't always easy. Satan is always at your shoulder, picking and teasing and trying to bring you down and there will be times when it will be very difficult to look at your situation positively.

And it doesn't help when you are surrounded by married couples and families. Here though, you will find things aren't as depressing as they might seem. Almost certainly you will find that you're not the only woman in your church who isn't married. It could even be that there are quite a few singles and solitaries for you to seek companionship with. In some situations you can find that the odd one out is the married person. At the time of writing I'm working as one of a team of five women with ages ranging from the late twenties to the late forties. Only one of us is married and the rest are completely single (that is, neither widowed nor divorced).

If you really yearn for a husband and children but they don't materialise, don't let yourself feel guilty for having wanted them. These are only natural desires after all. Eventually you will channel your life into other areas and, as time goes on, if these other areas are really the things God has led you to, you will find them deeply satisfying and come to realise that perhaps you weren't cut out for marriage and motherhood anyway. Or perhaps you are simply marked down for a later than average marriage. After all, there's no arbitrary age for it. Who says you have to be settled by thirty, forty, fifty or more. In my own situation I can now look back and see how disastrous it would have been for me to have married in my twenties. I just wasn't ready. And I've got no doubt that if I had married then, I would now either be divorced or enduring a very unhappy plight. But, as with so many other things with God, it takes time. Time to heal you of your desperation and time to discover the path that you should be on. So give God the time. Be patient. Trust him. He won't fail you.

Bereft

Grief, like most other things in life, will have an effect on you that is entirely personal. But there is one golden rule that you would do well to follow. Let yourself feel it. If you are mourning the loss of a loved one – your husband, a relative or close friend – don't let anyone tell you that you 'should be over it by now' when you so clearly aren't. And ignore that famous line, 'Pull yourself together'. Such phrases, even when well meant, denote a fault in the speaker's attitude rather than in your response to your situation.

With the best will in the world I can only write about bereavement in a way that will seem fairly clinical even though, for you, that subject may be charged with unutterable depths of emotion. However, if you are going through, or have been through, such a time the last thing you'll want to read is a series of platitudes which will probably not have any bearing on your particular circumstances.

The thing is, grieving is a necessary and normal part of the healing process involved in coping with loss. It is as essential in the emotional (and mental) sense, as a scab forming over a cut is in the physical. It is a vital preliminary to learning to live without that person and eventually (when you're stronger – and you will be) to letting the loved one go, to saying goodbye to them.

It doesn't help to be given clever-sounding facts like 'grief is really self-pity' and 'we mourn for ourselves, not for the departed one'. It may be true but that doesn't make your pain any less real, or make it go away any quicker. It doesn't even mean that it's less deserving of God's healing touch. It does mean, however, that the person saying it isn't particularly sensitive to your needs at that moment.

And that brings me to another thing about grief. The need to share it. I don't mean by that that you want to make everybody else as miserable as you, but a shoulder to cry on will prove invaluable here. Someone with whom you can let go. It's said that in times of trouble you find out who your friends are (or 'a friend in need is a friend indeed' if you like). It's true. And in the future when you look back on your time of sadness you will note and remember with affection those who stood by you when you were low, who made you endless cups of tea and sat up late with you while you poured out your woe. They will also be the ones who listened with a great deal of sympathy and didn't say much. They won't be the people who told you to 'buck up' and to 'try not to think about it'.

As I say, let yourself go through it. Everything in creation moves in procession. The first shock of bereavement is often a kind of numbness. Almost like an emotional anaesthetic. Then, when the loss hits, there follows a period of mourning, of grieving. After that, in some cases a long while after, comes the time when the bereaved find that they begin to let the loved one go, to say goodbye and to start rebuilding their lives without that person. It may seem strange to talk about 'letting someone go' when that someone is dead but it can often be that, inside yourself you haven't released the departed one. You haven't accepted their death. In some cases it can be quite acute . . . 'I just know he's going to come through that door again' . . . And if it's like that for you, don't worry. The healing process is different in everyone and eventually, as the pain diminishes, you will find yourself picking up the pieces of your life, or even discovering a whole new world.

It will seem like a double blow to you if, as well as the pain of your bereavement, you are now having to face the future alone. Try not to panic. Panic never serves anyone. In fact, try not to think about the future. It's in good hands already and at the moment you have enough on your plate to get through each day. And that's how you should take it. Moment by moment. All you have to concentrate on is your next task or requirement. And whether the next thing is to sit down and have a good cry or hoover the living-room carpet you don't have to think beyond that.

Then there is another aspect to coping with death that you may feel need of. This is entirely personal but you might feel that you want to take one last look at the body of the dead person. They might still be in the bed where they died, at the mortuary or 'laid out' in the chapel of rest at the undertakers. Whatever the case, if you feel the need to see them then do so. Don't let anyone persuade you out of it with reasonings such as, 'It will only upset you more,' and 'It's best to remember them as they were.' You know what you feel and your need to see your loved one in death can be very much a part of the letting go, and therefore healing, process. When my father died it was something none of my family even needed to speak about to each other. Not because it was taboo but because it was unnecessary. As each brother who wasn't staying at my parents' house at the time arrived, they automatically did what the rest of us had already done, which was to go into the bedroom to see Dad. Even now, I believe it was something that was necessary and that if I hadn't gone in to see him I would still feel the lack of that action.

In a way, even though we don't use the same terms you can go through more or less the same grieving process if your husband has left you or if your boyfriend has told you that it's all over.

Here, though, the pain is different because the loved one is still around; they might even be sharing their life with somebody else.

At least in the case of the dead person you know they have gone for good. And you can console yourself that they died in the love you always shared between you and carried that love to Heaven with them.

But with an absent husband or boyfriend it is the love which you once shared that has died. At least it has died in them.

This is particularly hurtful and damaging to your confidence. If you still have the same strong feelings for them that you've always had, you will spend a long time in hoping that they will come back to you; and in trying to get them back.

Sometimes there is a happy ending. A couple can discover that all they needed was a bit of breathing space and an opportunity to clear their heads. And they come together renewed and refreshed and stronger than ever before.

But as we know only too well, and as divorce statistics tragically testify, this isn't always the case. And in these instances the abandoned partner will eventually have to let go and seek to build up a life alone.

For many Christians this is likely to mean facing up to the rest of your life being lived as a single person, and if you find yourself in this situation you will need all the support that can be given by your church community, your family and your friends.

Some Christian communities take a less strict line than others on divorce and remarriage, which is not only unbiblical but it can lead to the scandal of couples 'shopping around' to find a church that will marry them. Of course this is a massive subject and since this is a book about living alone and not about marriage I don't propose to go into it. Suffice to say that for many Christians, the break up of a marriage, and all the problems and heartbreak that that entails will go hand in hand with facing the future alone.

Peter Bye

*Peter Bye, born in London in 1938, started his working
career as an office boy at Chappell's, the music publisher.
Now he works as a freelance arranger/composer/record
producer/musical director and occasionally as a pianist.*

I started living alone because I had to, and I live alone now
because, on balance, I choose to. I had to because I was
divorced, but now I've got my head together again and all
the emotions have died down and things are quieter, I find
– partly because of what I do for a living – that I'm mostly
happier on my own. Just once in a while it would be nice if
somebody else was around, but that's maybe two days out
of seven, which isn't a good foundation for living with
someone.

When you live with somebody, you have to impose a
certain amount of self-discipline to make it work. If you live
on your own there are areas where you can be incredibly
selfish. And that, depending on the sort of person you are,
can either be very bad for you or it can be very good,
because apart from those areas you may become much more
long-suffering and easy to get on with.

Occasionally, living on my own, I get very lonely and
very introspective. If there are times when there's not a lot
of work about, I start to realise how tenuous one's hold is
on health and sanity and everything else, and it has made
me realise how much, in fact, I rely on God every day to
keep me together. When there are a lot of people around,
and there's plenty to do, I find it very easy to kid myself
that I'm coping with life well and it would take a lot to make
me crack. But it only needs a couple of evenings on my own
with nothing much on television and no book in the house

that I feel like reading, and I realise how tenuous my hold on stability really is.

I think, on balance, that living alone is a help as far as my spiritual life goes. There is no point in my praying or reading the Bible immediately when I get out of bed in the morning; it takes an hour and a half before I'm in touch with the world or anything at all. Which means that somewhere else in the day I've got to fit in that time of study and contemplation, and if there's somebody else around then it becomes incredibly difficult. There is an obligation to them to fit in with their life-styles. So I think that probably, in that sense, being on my own is a help.

As for feeling lonely, I would say that the loneliness I feel now is a negative loneliness. I'm on my own and there's nobody around, so I feel very . . . *yeuk*. But then, when you're married and the marriage isn't working, you've got all the disadvantages of living with somebody plus the loneliness. It's a sort of active loneliness. You've got none of the compensations of living with somebody else but all the drawbacks.

To me, loneliness is just a longing for the company of other people. I mentioned two days out of seven earlier, but I don't feel real loneliness as often as that. On these two days probably I think, 'Hey, it would be nice if somebody else was around' or 'I've cooked too much . . . somebody else could eat half of it,' and silly things like that. It would be nice when watching a television programme to be able to ask, 'What do you think of that?' But real, deep loneliness when I think, 'Oh, I do wish there was somebody else here. I feel I need somebody around . . .', that happens a day a month probably, at the outside.

Some people who dread living on their own will actually find, when they do it, that it is not so bad. There are good things to be said about it. Others will find it fulfils all their worst dreams. I would hesitate to advise anybody on the matter unless I felt I knew them very, very well. For me, because a lot of my work is writing, I sit there, twelve hours a day sometimes, writing. And because I'm concentrating on my work, I'm not conscious of being alone. And at the end of twelve hours' writing there's not a lot of the day left. So in one sense I'm insulated against loneliness far more than most people. Writing is, by its nature, solitary. But you don't feel solitary, you're tied up, you're occupied.

I think loneliness sometimes comes not just from being alone, but because when we're alone there's a sense of insecurity, in creative people especially. They have to keep bouncing their personality off other people and seeing the echoes come back and assuring themselves that they're all right, that they're not as bad as they think they are. And if you get in a situation where there aren't people around and you're not experiencing that image of yourself coming back at you, you tend to lose your identity. Being artistic is a very insecure way of life, and not having that reassurance of somebody reflecting your own image back to you all the time can be very destructive.

When it comes to other people's attitudes to me as a person living alone, there's no problem. I've been a musician all my life so I'm used to being looked at fairly strangely by the people who think there's something odd about not having your insurance cards stamped for you or going to work on the same train at the same time every day. The comments I get most often are from the non-Christian people I work with when I'm in the studios and so on. 'Oh, you're living on your own? Cor, I bet you have a marvellous time, wish I was on me own . . .' And I can see, from their point of view, if you're living with someone, the attraction of feeling, 'Boy, if I was on my own that would be really terrific . . . I could have a different girl friend every night.' When it actually comes to it, when you *are* on your own and you've done the cooking and the washing-up and the housework, you've got no strength left. You think about phoning somebody and you decide, 'Oh no, it's too much hassle,' and you just collapse in front of the television set.

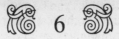

6

The men in your life

You might think there aren't any. But there probably are. Just because you don't have a particular man friend at the moment it doesn't mean that you have no relationships at all with the opposite sex. Even if you have no close male friends, one or two men may very well be numbered among your acquaintances. If you are thinking, 'Oh yes but I wasn't counting those,' then that's exactly the type of attitude I was thinking of when I was talking about relationships at the beginning of chapter 2.

Some women have very little experience of men. They come from all-girl families or maybe were only children. They might have had brothers but been educated away from home so that they never had much to do with them.

I remember once working in a shipping company (oh, the roving life of a temp!). The office was full of men, and one afternoon a woman who worked on a lower floor came up on some business. She was unmarried and gave the general impression that she had had rather a sheltered upbringing. As she passed me on her way back to her own floor she smiled pleasantly and said, 'How do you like working with all these *men*?' The tone of her voice on the word 'men' implied 'these strange and alien creatures'. Her general demeanour was rather quaint, and although I don't think many women really regard men in this light any more, nonetheless it taught me that not everyone had grown up like I had (football and cricket were never a problem, but I just couldn't get the hang of that stupid game netball).

Most people are aware nowadays of how our upbringing

affects us; of how attitudes passed on to us get stuck in and influence our thinking for the rest of our lives. I don't think that having five brothers has given me a better or worse outlook on men than a woman with, say, five sisters. It does mean that I'm probably less surprised by them but even that doesn't necessary give me more (or less) successful relationships.

Suffice it to say that your men friends can be great mates and every bit as valuable as your female friends. If you limit yourself to thinking that there's only one kind of alliance a woman can have with a man, then you will be denying yourself what might be some very solid and worthwhile relationships.

Looking for marriage

Yes, well this is a most understandable temptation, and I don't suppose there's a woman (or a man for that matter) who hasn't experienced it. You'll probably have heard all the good advice about how you shouldn't regard each man you meet as a potential husband and of course you know how sensible and right it is.

Knowing all this though isn't of much help in doing it; especially at times when you're feeling particularly low about being unmarried. No doubt you will be praying for release (though that in itself is a hard thing to do sometimes). But if you feel you're guilty of 'husband hunting' it might be of assistance to you to do what I recommended earlier for shyness. When you're talking to a man, try to imagine what you look like. Listen to yourself. And try to reverse the situation. That is, try to imagine what your reaction would be if a man approached you with a similar attitude to that with which you approach men. If you're honest the chances are that you'll be able to admit that a man who treats every woman as a potential wife would make you want to run a mile. So why should a man be different? Why should he be drawn to any woman 'with her claws out'?

Another thing is that it's not flattering. A man like that

wouldn't make you think, 'Wow! he thinks I'm great.' In reality you would know that it would be more a case of, 'He's talking to me because I'm the nearest/most eligible female here.' Or even, 'What a muggins I am, fancy getting lumbered in conversation with this wimp.' Again, why should men be any different?

If you're feeling desperate at the moment you have my deepest sympathy. If it's a particularly trying time for you it might help you to know that one day you'll find that you're not looking for a partner any more. This won't necessarily be because you'll have found one but because you'll have ceased to worry over the issue. Either suddenly, or over a long period of time, the burden will have been taken from you and you'll have been brought to realise that life isn't yours to dictate and you have every reason to be joyful regardless of whether or not you're sharing it with anyone.

No room for a man

Far from grasping at every man they meet some women actually recoil from them. And it's quite a curious thing but you can jog happily along in your life for some considerable time without realising that there might be anything odd or even unhealthy in your attitude to men.

In a way, a Christian can be more at risk here than a person with no particular religious conviction. It's very simple. The Christian is required to abstain from sexual intercourse before marriage and so a repressed person, or somebody with some form of sexual problem, is probably less likely to find themselves in a situation where they are expected to indulge. They might think that their abstinence is due to the high moral code by which they live. But in fact, living by a high moral code can be a welcome, though unconscious, camouflage for a distinct distaste for, or fear of, sex.

Naturally I'm not advocating fornication as the antidote to any problem you may have. But even if you never marry, it ought to be for the right reasons and not the wrong ones.

65

God invented sex, after all. He could have arranged it so that babies *were* found in cabbage patches, or that storks flew around the sky with us hanging in cloths from their bills. But he didn't. So even though you are expected to practise chastity it cannot serve either God, the community at large or yourself to have anything other than a healthy, relaxed and God-inspired attitude to sex and sexuality.

There are all sorts of reasons why people have bad attitudes towards sex. It may be something relatively easy to trace. Perhaps, in an effort to get you to 'behave yourself' your parents have somehow passed on the idea that sex is evil. Or there's the famous one that 'all men are only after one thing' and therefore they ought to be held rigidly at bay. It could even be that you've simply never met anybody who turned you on.

If you are able to recognise that a problem exists and can be honest and open, then it should be easy to deal with. You probably won't have to do anything drastic like seeking specialised help. Simply through prayer and the gradual opening up of your mind to an examination of what exactly the trouble is and how it might have come about, you will be set on the road.

Sometimes you may find it helpful to ease your problem into a conversation, just to see what others may think. You don't even have to own up to the fact that it's yourself you are talking about. A chat with your cleric or an older woman at your church might also be of assistance. This could be especially helpful if, in opening up your mind you are frightened, deep down, that you are in danger of becoming 'impure'. The authoritative voice of your church should be of great comfort here. (Though it's as well to remember that some church groups seem to be, in themselves, quite repressed on the subject of sex and sexuality. If this is the case you should seek counsel from elsewhere within the Christian community.) Remember, nobody is trying to threaten your faith or chastity. But having a thoroughly healthy attitude to everything, under God, is only what's desirable and proper for the Christian and any blockage, for that is what it is, prevents a healthy flow. One half of the human race is, after all, male, and anything which cuts them off from you (unless you're a nun, which is an entirely different situation and not at all applicable here) cannot be a good thing.

Of course, your problem could be far more deeply rooted and spring from some particular and devastating trauma. Perhaps you were raped or sexually abused as a child (or even later in life). Perhaps a member of your family forced you to commit incest, which is a lot more common than many people think. The effects of these and similar acts can warp a person for many years after the offences themselves, and it's very possible that those around you are likely to be unable to supply the expert help you need. If your problem seems to be deep-rooted you are advised to seek specialist help. It might not even appear to be sexual. All sorts of apparently unrelated neuroses can arise from one individual problem, but you can receive help and I can only advise you not to delay in availing yourself of it.

Starstruck

This is one we all know something about. At one time or another we have all swooned over some pop singer/actor/sports star. It's perfectly normal; it's even healthy. The phenomenon is usually accompanied by teenage spots and puppy-fat. If, as we grow, we continue to be fans of a particular personality our devotion often widens and matures into a genuine appreciation and admiration of that person both as a performer and a human being. Even here it isn't necessarily a bad thing. Indeed it can be quite the opposite.

But it is also possible that the person of whom you are a devoted fan has become 'the man in your life'. This is the man that fills your waking hours. You look in clothes shops with an eye to what would suit him. You know exactly the food he likes to eat (and the food you think he should be

67

eating). And you spend a prodigious amount of time and money going to where this person will be. This doesn't mean that there's something wrong with you. In fact you could be very clear-headed on the subject. It may be that, yes, he is the only man in your life: yes, that's the way you like things; and no, you wouldn't be particularly open to any other offers even if you weren't a fan of this person. It is important to note here that not all dedicated fans follow their idol with the hope of special notice or even marriage in mind. The majority of fans of most stars are well-adjusted people with boyfriends/husbands/families or plenty of other people and interests in their lives. But it can sometimes happen that this isn't the case, and a healthy appreciation of someone can become an unhealthy obsession. Do you, for instance, have only one topic of conversation – your idol? Do you fantasise constantly about him? Do you measure all men up against him? In fact can you honestly say that your devotion to this person is not preventing you from forming other relationships?

It could even be linked with a problem mentioned in the previous section, in that your fear or distaste for men (and what they mean in terms of sex) has led you to substitute the men who are available for one who isn't – one who will always have to be, in some way, distant from you. Only you can know if your devotion to a famous person goes over the top. And only you, by God's grace, can do anything about it.

Jenny Cook

Jenny Cook was born at Croydon in 1944. She started her working career as a secretary at the BBC. She later went to the Christian magazine Crusade *(now called* Today*) and later still, to TEAR Fund (The Evangelical Alliance Relief Fund). She is now the membership secretary of the Arts Centre Group, an organisation catering for the needs of Christians in the arts and the media.*

When I left home I moved into a flat and shared for about seven years. When you're younger, that's great. But, as a woman, you need to create your own home and that can often cause tensions if you're sharing with somebody else who has different ideas from you, or if you've got to share a small space. So I moved into an unfurnished flat and then, eventually, bought my own.

It took a little while to adapt. In the unfurnished flat I was living on my own, but in a house with other people, and that was really good because there was always somebody around if I needed them. And then I bought my own place; and I shut my front door and there was nobody else there. That was quite an odd feeling. Once I got to know the neighbours it was great, and fortunately it didn't take too long to get to know them. But when you first move into your own place you feel, There's nobody I can actually go to. Not that you necessarily have to go to anybody. It's just knowing that somebody's there if you wanted to. But when I got to know the neighbours, as I said, it was fine.

I'm sure other people have said that if you live on your own you become very selfish because you've only got yourself to please and there isn't anybody else there who you can relate to or talk to. From that point of view, I hope it hasn't made me selfish, but it may have because I've got so used to being on my own and thinking of just what I want to do rather than think of other people. The other way it might have changed me is that you have to be sociable if there's somebody else there when you get in at night or you're having a meal together, but now I'm living alone it may be that I have an evening when I hide away from people a bit and don't make the effort to go out because it's rather nice to be on my own.

Unless you've lived on your own you're not going to understand other people who do. And I can see the point of view of other people who find it very difficult. Personally I don't, except if I'm feeling very low, or perhaps when I'm ill, which is another issue. But I can now sympathise with people who can't cope with it and who perhaps find it very, very difficult not to be married or not to share a home. Because you have to go out to make your entertainment, to see people. It doesn't happen automatically; I have learned that. But also, I think I've learned not to be afraid of being alone, but to really enjoy it. Because I do enjoy it. If you're very busy in a job during the day, just to have space to yourself when you get in is very important, particularly, I think, for a woman.

I do fear growing old alone. When I was younger I didn't think about it very much. But I'm in my forties now, and one thing I do find about being alone is that you begin to imagine you've got things wrong with you. There was a time when I'd been going through quite a difficult patch for about a year and had been under a lot of pressure at work. That had a physical effect eventually, and I started to worry about my health. At the moment I'm fine, and I'm not worrying. But I've been through those stages of feeling very low and immediately thinking the worst. It's completely irrational. I looked back on it afterwards and thought, that was crazy! So yes, I am afraid . . . of being afraid, but then I'm a very fearful person. I'm very afraid of change, and that's just a part of my personality which I try to fight against.

Personally, I find being alone very difficult spiritually because I love to pray with other people. It's very hard to pray on your own and to discipline yourself about it. When I've lived with other Christians in the past, of course that's easier, because then you can share things, or you can pray together and that helps you and builds you up as a Christian. So the actual living on your own, I think, is hard spiritually. Particularly if you're really tired or depressed or low, and that is the last time you really want to pray, and there's nothing to spur you on. It's the kind of person I am, because I enjoy being very busy and I actually don't find it easy to sit and do nothing.

I would define loneliness as feeling completely cut off – I think you can be very lonely in a crowd of people, when you're not relating to what's going on around you – not relating to the people. Really, I think you can be loneliest in a crowd.

It must be very, very hard, if you've been married, to have to live alone. I find it a joyful thing because my home is something I've been given by God. But I think the advice I would give to anybody who was having to live alone would be, Give it time. That's a practical thing. Because I'm sure, after any kind of relationship breaking up, whether you've been sharing with friends or you've been married, it does take time to adjust. But I would also say, Don't be afraid of it, because it is a gift that God gives you.

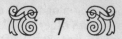

7

Being Martha when you want to be Mary

Right then, first things first. For whatever reason, you're living on your own. If you haven't already realised it you are about to learn that you can no longer spend as much on clothes, make-up and socialising as you used to. You have now discovered a whole new set of priorities for the use of your hard-earned money. The next chapter goes into this in more detail. But meanwhile, here are some practical tips.

The first of these is the most obvious. Having acquired a roof over your head, you have to hang on to it. This means paying either rent or a mortgage. I was once given a very good piece of advice on this issue which applies equally well to both and, though it may seem like stating the obvious, I don't know that it is to everybody so I'll throw it in for good measure.

'Always pay your rent,' I was told. 'Whatever else, pay your rent. If money's tight the lady next door will give you a cup of sugar. Someone else will give you an egg or two and one of the other neighbours will part with a few slices of bread. But nobody is going to pay your rent for you.'

Try to regard your rent money as untouchable, taboo. It's very easy, especially if you've got a jolly and friendly landlord/lady to be lackadaisical; but it can get you into trouble. What about such a situation as this? There's a lovely dress in the High Street that you want but can't really afford. So you decide to use the rent money to pay for it and pay double the rent next week, by which time your friend Jane will have paid you back that twenty quid she owes you. It all sounds very casual and easy going and might even work.

But, just as easily, it could lead to disaster. It's quite possible that, come next week, Jane will only be able to pay you half, or will even ask you if you can wait a further week (as she's got to pay the rent). It's then that you discover that landlords, even the jolly and friendly ones, tend to have this strange, morbid obsession with getting their rent paid.

So there's your mortgage or rent to be deducted from your wages or salary. Then there are those other little matters of keeping warm, and having enough light to see by, and being able to pick up a telephone and call somebody when you need a chat. I'm fully behind the notion that the best things in life are free but, clearly, some of the most necessary aren't. Like it or lump it, household bills are going to drop through your letterbox with monotonous regularity every quarter. Different people have different ways of paying them. Some arrange standing orders or direct debits with their banks. Others like to put money by in a building society so that it can build up a little interest before being used.

On the question of paying bills, though, you would be wise to wait and consider a while before opening any budget accounts or buying stamps each week for use in paying a bill later. Charges for telephone, gas, electricity and rates are quite high enough so why should we give these organisations more money than we have to. Take the case of buying telephone stamps for instance. This is mooted as a very convenient way of saving for your next bill, and indeed does work like that. But look at what else it does. For one thing, you're now paying your bill before you've got it, therefore before you need to. More than that, though, you're helping British Telecom to make a nice fat profit from you without even trying. It's very simple. You may only buy one fifty-pence stamp each week. That's not much of course, but it only needs two or three million people across the country to buy a fifty-pence telephone stamp each week and there's one to one and a half milllion pounds worth of interest-earning capital going into the coffers of British Telecom (who are laughing all the way to the bank). The important thing to remember is that money grows. It makes more money. And why should your telephone stamp money earn interest for British Telecom when it could be earning interest for you in your own building society account?

The golden rule to remember is that any scheme which is suggested to you to help make paying your bills easier is more likely to work in favour of the body you're paying rather than you. Considering the vast profits they make and the fact that charges *never* go down, I personally don't see why they should get any more of our money than we can help.

Once you've been on your own for a few months you'll probably find that you've got an idea of how much to save and how much you can spend and you'll relax somewhat on the question of money. Whatever your situation though, unless living alone also coincided with starting a fantastic new job, the chances are you'll discover that you're not as well off as you were when living with your parents or when you were sharing a flat. This prospect may sound awful, especially if you thought you were already poor enough. But after a while you'll realise that your flat hasn't been repossessed by the mortgage company (or alternatively you haven't been evicted for non-payment of rent). You have clothes on your back, food in your stomach and you can still afford to socialise, even if that socialising is rather a scaled-down version from formerly.

Of course, money apart, there will be another reason why your socialising may be somewhat curtailed.

Head cook and bottle washer

'I'm sorry I can't come out tonight, I'm washing my hair,' is a traditional excuse/reason for spending an evening indoors.

Living on your own you will find it becomes, 'I'm sorry I can't come out tonight, I've got to wash my floor (or windows, or clothes or . . .)' Yes, unfortunately the house-work doesn't do itself.

If you've been living with your family or with other people it's possible you might not have discovered some of the short cuts.

For instance, you may still be full of good intentions about getting up nice and early, leaving the place spick and span and making sure the breakfast things are washed, dried and put away before you go to work. You would be wise however, before you plunge into the washing up of that one cup, plate, knife, fork and spoon to stop and consider the matter. Such discipline is admirable and I certainly wouldn't knock it, but just think a moment. Washing up liquid and hot water both cost money, your money since it's you paying all the bills now. Is one cup, plate, knife, fork and spoon worth the expenditure? Why not wait until after your main meal, then at least you'll have a bowlful.

And speaking of main meals. What a drag having to come home after a hard day's work and start cooking. I am now in the happy position of being in a job where I get a full meal provided in the middle of the day. This is nothing short of manna from Heaven as far as I'm concerned. It leaves me free in the evenings to just have some fruit with a sandwich or a few slices of toast if I feel hungry, and is a terrific saving on my food bills, not to mention what I gain through not having to turn on my own cooker and use up expensive fuel.

And though this chapter isn't about your work situation as such, since I'm on on the subject of food I think this is a good time to pause and consider the staff restaurant/ canteen, if you have one. I realise some companies' catering facilities have an appalling reputation and only you can know if the one at your place of work deserves it. Financi-ally, however, the fact is that if your company provides either free, or generously subsidised, meals you may find that the salaries they pay are lower than you could get for doing the same job elsewhere. This may sound like a minus, but the point I'm trying to make is that if you can get cheap or free food at work then it can be worth up to about £1,000 a year on your wages. Of course, if you're thinking of your mortgage rating you may need that £1,000 on your pay slip and not in your stomach. But my point still carries. It *could* be worth your while to be in a slightly less well paid job. Naturally, for us as Christians, our first priority in taking a new job or leaving an old one is obedience to the Lord. However, if you're puzzled as to why he seems to be leading you to the one with less money up front it's as well to know what compensations may be following on behind.

Before I settled where I am (thankfully a job which also allows me time to write), I moved around a great deal as a temp for many years. I've seen quite a few staff canteens in my time, and on the whole I would say that they provide nourishing, well-balanced meals. In my experience it seems that the powers that be in the kitchens are manifestly aware of their workers' need for a good selection of green vegetables and salads as well as protein.

If your company has a staff canteen you would be very wise to make full use of it. Eating in the middle of the day also means that you'll use up the energy from the food as the rest of the day wears on, which I gather is better for the figure (those on a diet take note!). And how much nicer, if you have an evening service, Mass, Bible study or some other church or social activity to attend, that you should be able to rest before leaving home instead of tearing along having been slaving over a hot stove, gulping down the meal and trying to get the washing-up done before setting out. Yes, I know the washing-up can be left until you get back, but who wants to start washing-up at the end of the evening? In the case of those who refrain from food before Communion, they have the additional problem of making sure they can eat early enough to keep a fast, or of not eating until afterwards.

If you haven't got a canteen at work you'll probably find that you go to the sandwich bar near your place of work.

This is not the ideal way to eat, and if you can find a good, reasonably priced restaurant it might be worth the expense to frequent it. You won't be losing all that much money actually, when you consider that the sandwiches you'll otherwise buy are not all that cheap (downright extortionate in some cases!), and again, you'll save on your home food/electric bills. Whatever you do, though, I don't suppose you need me to tell you about the need for fresh fruit and green vegetables in your diet.

But wait! Do I hear you cry? Doesn't this woman know about making up a few sandwiches or a salad the night before? That way you save all round.

The answer is yes, I do know all about that. I've even done it. But I found that those good intentions never lasted longer than a few days before I was back in the sandwich-bar queue.

I have now said quite a bit about how to wheedle out of doing any more cooking than you have to. However, in your situation, you may have no alternative (or you just might not be the wheedling type). If you have no choice but to make yourself a main meal when you get home of an evening there are still ways in which the work involved can be cut to a minimum, at least during the week when time is at a premium. Yes, I know all time belongs to the Lord, but does it serve your relationship with him if eight or nine o'clock at night is the earliest you can sit down and relax? Sitting down to rest and renew ourselves is as important to our spiritual lives as is going about our allotted tasks with joy at doing his bidding.

So here we go then. I'm a vegetarian, so can't speak about how quickly or easily a meat meal can be turned out – though I believe, from the things I hear, that since meat is expensive it's not something even you carnivores can afford to have every day. There are, however, several alternatives. Please don't throw up your gastronomically purist hands in horror at this but there are some quite healthy things being put into tins these days. I've often bought tinned macaroni cheese for instance, and though I'm not about to advertise, a quick look at some of the labels will tell you which ones have no preservatives, additives or colouring. Then there's lentil soup, full of protein and, being a legume, fibre. So is pease pudding; I used to pop a fried egg on top of a dollop of pease pud with some ketchup, or you can easily spice up the taste, if desired, with some curry powder or herbs. Then of course there are eggs or cheese on their own. All these things are full of protein.

As for the rest of the main meal, summer and winter a salad is better for you than cooked vegetables. If you feel you need more bulk, the sort of thing which, if you had more time, or felt like it, you would get from potatoes, then a slice or two of wholemeal bread should serve you. Sometimes in the past I've also bought myself a tin of hummous (delicious) and pitta bread. Hot pitta bread dipped in hummous and served with a salad used to be one of my treats. Then there's Old Faithful, the ubiquitous baked bean. Full of protein and fibre, baked beans are unquestionably nourishing.

I'm only making a few suggestions; you can probably come up with others. The point is that very little time is needed to prepare the things I've suggested and they require only a minimum of effort and fuel. Another plus of course is that if all you have to cook on is a single gas ring or electric plate then you can hardly be juggling with recipes which require you to be bringing the cheese sauce to the boil just as the cauliflower is getting tender at the same time as the potato croquettes are ready.

As for sweets, apart from a particular occasion when it is nice to do something special you can consider them irrelevant. A piece of fruit will do you more good. Assuming you are getting all the protein, vitamins and fibre you need from the main course then a sweet, though pleasant, is unnecessary. Personally I only ever exert myself to make a sweet dish when I have guest, and even then I sometimes cheat by serving up a nice and easy fruit salad.

And the in-between maid

When it comes to the other household jobs, tedious as they are, they've just got to be done. It can be quite depressing, not to mention counter-productive, to try to relax in front of the television when you can see a layer of dust around or if the room or the carpet is groaning under the weight of the accumulated fluff and debris. You'll soon realise, though, that most of these jobs in themselves don't take up much time, and the dirt and dust can be kept down fairly easily. Of course we all know someone who washes all the woodwork down every week or who is equally assiduous at some other task which could quite well be left for reasonably long intervals. Personally, I find that I'm long past the stage of being intimidated by such bizarre behaviour and rarely feel even a twinge of guilt about what life-forms might be lurking at the back of my cupboard or under the cooker.

Of all household chores one of the most horrible is the laundry. If you have no washing machine then you'll find the local launderette a great boon here. I used to hate these places with a passion that led me to doing all my washing by hand at home. However I've recently become reconciled to them, and now I even find trips to my local one quite interesting. After all, you meet all sorts of people in them. But if you can't easily get to a launderette or, like me in the past, absolutely hate to spend any time in one, then, if you can't afford a washing machine, at least try to get yourself a spin dryer. A spin dryer cuts out all the need to hang dripping wet clothes over the bath – especially a bonus if you share a bathroom with several others in the house.

After winter can spring be far away? And after the washing of course, comes the ironing. This is one of the other most horrible jobs. Those living alone can find themselves very much at an advantage when it comes to the ironing. That is, you can more or less dump this job with impunity. It's very simple. You don't actually have to iron anything until you are going to wear it (or the night before).

So that's it. Goodbye piles of ironing. Of course, not everybody chooses this easy option. I've heard of people who even iron their socks! (Yes, I could hardly believe it either.) I know another who irons sheets . . . well, each to their own I suppose, but why make work for yourself?

The prospect of fitting in the housework with a full-time job may seem a little daunting at first but you'll soon find that you're in the way of it.

Home sweet home

It may only be a scruffy bedsit, and you may hate having to live there; but don't let that deter you from making it as homely as you can. If you are living in furnished accommodation, that may seem a tall order as there are probably rules against decorating the place, banging nails in the walls or putting up shelves.

But there's nothing to stop you displaying your own ornaments on the mantle, your own choice of rug in front of the fireplace and your own cushions on the bed or easy chair.

When I lived in a bedsit I tried to maintain an attitude which made one end of the room the 'living-room' and the other end the 'bedroom'. Even if you don't like the furniture there's no reason why you can't distribute it according to your own taste. And it's amazing the difference you can make to a drab settee just by throwing a bright, cheerful blanket, length of fabric or even a curtain over it. As for the bed; why should it look like a bed when you're not actually sleeping in it? If you have a duvet you can roll it up under whatever covering you have to give an oriental divan look, and if you have blankets then you can hide the pillow and scatter yet more cushions around during the daytime.

There are all sorts of things you can do to make a place seem more cosy and reflective of your personality. In fact, the Lord being sufficient unto the day, your time spent in drab surroundings could bring out a vein of creativity in you that you never thought existed.

Pauline Webb

Pauline Webb, the daughter of a Methodist Minister, was born at Wembley in Middlesex. Although she began her career as a teacher she now works as a writer and broadcaster with the BBC. In addition to this she has written film scripts and is the author of several books on religious subjects. Apart from her professional life she is a Methodist lay preacher and in 1965 was elected vice-chairman of the Methodist Conference. She is also very well known for her work in high posts on the various committees of the World Council of Churches.

Living alone was for me a deliberate decision. I lived at home with my parents for as long as I could, then I bought my own flat. I haven't married; I suppose that's partly through choice. But it wasn't a definite decision that I wanted to be single. It was just that the choice of marriage was never one that I, at that particular time, wanted to accept.

It didn't take me as long as I expected to adapt. I had had a very good home life with my parents, and I actually moved out when they were old, not because I wanted to desert them, of course, but because I felt it was necessary to move into my own home and keep up a close relationship with them before they died. I thought that the trauma of bereavement and then being alone all at once would be too much and so, in a way, I had a half-way stage when I lived very near to them but I did have my own flat. Therefore, in a sense, I eased myself into the situation of being alone. So, at one time I was running around visiting them a lot, and then when they had gone of course there was all the grief and bereavement, but at least I was used to the fact that I could come back to my own place.

Living alone has caused a lot of changes in me. I think it makes you very much more self reliant. You tend to become tidier, in a funny way, because you know that if you don't put things away nobody else is going to do it. Everything remains in the house exactly as it was when you left it; so when you come back it's your fault if it's untidy. I think one of the most interesting things about living alone is that you have no one else to blame for anything that goes wrong. And rather like a small child who kicks the table when she knocks her head against it, I think even a lot of adults look for someone else to blame if they lose something or something gets broken or they've forgotten where it is. When you live alone you can't do that. You have to admit, 'I must have put it down in a foolish place or I must have lost it.' And that's good in a way, because it makes you take responsibility for your actions. It makes you a bit more lenient towards yourself and it makes you more lenient towards other people.

I've learnt how important friendships are and how necessary it is that you keep your friendships in repair. When you live alone you haven't any relationships that are there by contract and which will continue whatever you do about them. So all your friendships are dependent upon your keeping contact with people. I don't mean you have to be constantly on the phone or writing letters, but I find I need friends a lot; I need the social contact with them. I have what I call my 'phone-in evenings' if I'm feeling particularly that I want to talk to people, when I ring several people. I think it is essential to have a telephone. It is important that you have these means of contact and do, in fact, use them; that you don't just sit down, if you are feeling particularly lonely or if there's something you very much want to talk over with someone. It's no use sitting there and fretting; 'Oh dear, I live alone . . . no one to talk to . . .' You need to take an initiative, and that either means phoning a friend or writing a letter or going to visit somebody or inviting somebody round.

It's made a difference to my spiritual life because I have found there's a need to develop inner resources. And in some ways it is easy to become more slack about that. We used to have family prayers every Sunday in my family home when I was a child and right up to my adult life. When that's gone, and you are on your own, obviously you don't make a ritual of always having the same kind of prayer time. I try daily to have some sort of clear time when I'm quiet and I pray, but it doesn't become so ritualistic as it was, because there's no one to check up on me and I'm not making any kind of public witness by what I'm doing. So it is really important to make your own disciplines, and that can be more difficult, but it becomes more necessary too.

Living alone, one gets far more sympathy than one deserves. People often feel sorry for me. But I think it's a very underrated way of living; there are a lot of benefits in living alone. It may not be the best possible way of life – I think the best possible way of life must be a happy marriage – but it's much better than an unhappy marriage and it's certainly much better than unhappily being alone. There are ways of living alone happily, and people often don't realise that. They often misunderstand what the problems are. They think it means that you're always feeling lonely; it isn't that at all. You can do things about loneliness. The feeling is much more that other people don't always recognise that you have, in fact, got your own home. They tend to expect you always to be the one to go visiting. I am sometimes asked, 'Are you going home for Christmas?' And I reply, 'I am home, this is home.' They seem to think you're in some sort of transit camp, and that you're really looking for someone to live with – for marriage or a companion. And, although as I say, I still think a happy marriage is probably the best possible form of life, I don't think that to be happily alone is only a second best. I think it *is* a second best, but it's a good second best.

I would define loneliness as a sense of having no one to share something with, and living alone doesn't necessarily mean that. You probably still have a whole circle of friends that you can share things with; and that's why you've got to take the initiative. Loneliness is different from solitude, of course. There are times when you feel lonely. For me, the worst times are after a party or after I've been together with people and done a lot of interesting things; if I've been away on holiday, or have been having a good discussion with people and come back to an empty house while other people are going back to their families. Or even after a service when there's been a lot of talk about family worship and they're all going home to their Sunday dinners. The one meal I hate having alone is Sunday dinner, but I find that hardly ever happens because I've either been preaching and I get invited to people's homes or other people who are also alone invite me. So I think loneliness is really to be seen in the context of social occasions. It's when other people are involved in some big social occasion and you go away from it to be alone, that you can be lonely.

As for growing old alone, I suppose everybody's afraid of it, really. I think growing old can be a positive thing, and I've met so many old people who live alone and who seem to have developed enormous resources that I admire them. One of the advantages of living alone before you're old is that you don't fear growing old as much as other people who are bereaved suddenly when they are reaching old age; you know that living on your own hasn't got all those terrors.

But of course, the awful thing about facing real old age and frailty and feebleness and even, perhaps, senility is that you wonder who is going to be there to care for you. On the other hand it's quite a release to think that you're not going to be dependent on anyone. There's no one to be dependent on, so something's got to happen that's going to solve that situation. You're not going to be a drag on your children because there aren't any children to be a drag on. So in one sense you're afraid but not perhaps as afraid as other people who've never lived alone.

If I had to advise anybody who was having to live alone

I would try to emphasise the positive things. You have a kind of freedom when you live alone – freedom to do your own thing. As someone once said, 'You can eat a whole packet of liquorice allsorts and nobody tells you you're greedy.' You've not got somebody all the time giving you advice and telling you you shouldn't do this and you shouldn't do that and asking you why you're doing it. You can do crazy things when you want. You can get up in the middle of the night and wash your hair at two o'clock in the morning without somebody asking you why – apart from disturbing the neighbours of course. But if there is a certain liberation in the sense that you are free to be yourself and do what you want to do, it has its terrors as well, and it can lead into self-centredness. My advice would be, 'Enjoy the freedom of it; look positively at it.' You can have the house exactly as you want it, you can have your own things around you. Enjoy all that, but don't let it become obsessive so that you become the centre of it all. Make sure that you keep the doors open to welcome other people, that you give hospitality and that you're not always on the receiving end of it. Because, when you live alone, people tend, very kindly, always to invite you to go and see them, and it is, I think, enormously important that you actually invite people to come and see you. It is good for you, and you may find that often you have a kind of haven to give them. In fact, in some ways people who've got large families may find your home the sort of place where they can be themselves with you and just talk and relax. They're your friends, it gives them a different context to be in. If you go to see them they're still (for instance) mum of a family. If they come to see you they're just your friend and they can relax and be themselves. That is quite a service you have to give.

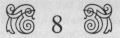

8

Money for your life

When it comes to talking about finances I have to confess
that I've passed the buck. I've off-loaded the responsibility
on to a good friend of mine who knows a lot more about it
than I do. So it's over to Michael McGowan BSc (Econ.)
for all the dirt on filthy lucre.

Almost no money

This chapter about money is for people with no, or almost
no money. If, then, you have bank or building society
accounts bursting with money, piles of bonds, a large
portfolio of unit trust, stocks and shares galore, a vast
pension fund and acres of freehold property, please *skip*
this chapter.

If, on the contrary, you rely entirely on state benefits and
do not expect that state of affairs to change, then this
chapter is not for you either except, perhaps, for the sections
on debts and house contents insurance.

No, this chapter is for people who earn a living, who are
concerned about finding enough to pay the bills, who never
have much, if any, money to spare and who always stop to
wonder whether they can afford it before making any
purchase which is not run of the mill.

Almost no answers

The good news is that there are a few books and some
regular publications written precisely for people who have
'almost no money'. There are also numerous organisations
which distribute free booklets; for example, the Stock

Exchange, banks, building societies, insurance companies, the Government and accountancy firms. Free advice can also be sought from places like the Citizens Advice Bureaux, the Department of Fair Trading, and Legal Advice Centres.

Some of these are listed at the end of this chapter. My aim here is simply to supplement the wealth of information available by helping you, if you live alone, to keep two things in mind when reading, or listening to, anything about money.

First: you probably have no one to fall back on in case of financial need.

Second: you are probably not too bothered about leaving a lot, or even any, money, to anyone else when you die.

If either of these sounds like you, then it should give you a different angle from people who do not live alone, on four money matters.

Nothing doing, doing nothing

(This is the tricky one; if you can cope with this the rest is plain sailing.)

It may seem somewhat premature to start thinking about retirement if you are at the beginning of your career, but planning your pension now is the most important financial decision you will have to make.

State retirement help for those who live alone in retirement is even worse than for married couples, and both are getting worse in real terms. Look at the table on page 88.

How would you cope with this drop in income if it happened to you tomorrow?

In fact, the reality may be even worse than the statistics suggest, for the same survey shows that people generally earn more between the ages of fifty and sixty-five than in early working life. The average, which includes all households, whether single person or not, shows that where the person (or head of household) is aged fifty to sixty-five, earnings are 10.07 per cent higher than in the average non-retired household.

TABLE
INCOME DROP AFTER RETIREMENT

Gross weekly income of single person households:

		Drop in weekly earnings	% of pre-retirement earnings received
Pre-retirement	£140.56		
Retired with own pension arrangements	£95.22	£45.34	68%
Retired and mainly dependent on state pensions	£43.19	£97.37	31%

Source: Government family expenditure survey 1985

So the average pre-retirement income of a single person is likely to be about £155 a week, which is over £100 more than the £43.19 'enjoyed' by the retired person mainly dependent on a state pension. Despite facts like these, most people do *nothing*, repeat *nothing*, about their retirement. If you are not convinced about this just telephone Help the Aged. They will tell you that there are nearly two million pensioners entirely dependent on supplementary benefit. Five to six hundred die each year from the cold and some die because they cannot afford a telephone to summon help in time.

Those who look forward to a 'government service' type of pension are reckoned to be fortunate. They expect a pension of two-thirds[1] of their final salary which, if they work for the Civil Service or the National Health Service, an Education Authority, a Local Authority or a large profitable company with a good pension scheme, is what they will receive so long as they work for the same employer for forty years or more. Even so, a vast number of employees of such organisations are quite ignorant of what are their benefits. All they have to do is ask for information.

If you are not in Government service or in something as

good as that, how much does it cost to set up for yourself such a scheme? Well, those in such schemes pay, or are deemed to pay, about 6 per cent of their salary. Imagine you are earning £140.56 per week about the time this book is published (the income quoted in the chart above) you are earning £101.86 a week more than the state pension of £38.70. Six per cent of that £140.56 is £8.43 a week. However, it is reckoned that the employer would need to add another 9 per cent, making 15 per cent in total, if the money all went into a real pension fund which would grow sufficiently to guarantee the benefits actually given[2], and, indeed, firms with 'good' pension schemes are usually looking at putting in a total of 15 per cent of salary which, in recent years with a healthy stockmarket, has given enough to provide additional benefits.

The 15 per cent for our example is £21.08 a week or £91.36 a month. Intriguingly, the maximum amount the Government permits employees already in company schemes to add to their own personal pension fund is 15 per cent, though for the self-employed the figure is 17½ per cent, of their earnings.

If £21.08 a week sounds rather a lot of money, relax, because to encourage people to save for retirement the Government allows tax relief on pension plans which, for someone putting in £21.08 a week, reduces the cost to £14.97 a week. In addition, the profits made by pension funds are free of tax so that the funds grow more quickly than other funds such as building society and insurance funds. Finally, you can withdraw approximately one-third of your pension fund tax free and possibly more than one-third if it is a company scheme. All in all, it is clearly a far better way to save money than the alternatives; though, of course, you cannot usually draw the benefits until retirement.

There are two other things which reduce the cost. The first is that if you are not in one of the big schemes (which are called 'contracted out' schemes) then you are 'included in' the basic state pension scheme to which your National Insurance contribution entitles you. In autumn 1986 this entitles those who have worked for forty years to £38.70 a week. If then, you are paying normal National Insurance contributions of £12.65 per week, then your pension contributions would be only 15 per cent of the difference between £38.70 and £140.56. After tax relief this reduces the cost from £14.97 a week to £10.85 a week.

Secondly, if you live alone you can reduce the cost even further by stating that you are not bothered about your relatives receiving anything if you die before retirement. If you start such a 'no return of fund' pension scheme then, if you die, instead of the fund going to your next of kin it would, in effect, be shared out among the other 'no return of fund' investors. In other words, if you are one of the fortunate ones to reach retirement you will have the same pension, but acquired more cheaply than someone who wants his fund to go to his spouse if he dies before retirement. Our mythical example putting in £10.85 a week from age twenty-five could probably obtain the same pension for about £8 a week from age twenty-five if she wants the pension to die with her.

If even that amount of about £1 a day is still too much, start *something*. Each year you delay you are a considerable step nearer to a poverty-stricken retirement. According to Abbey Life's figures, if a pension fund grows at only 10 per cent, then someone who starts a £30-a month return of fund pension plan at the age of twenty-nine can look forward to a fund, at age sixty-five, of £89,583; delay the start for a year and the fund at sixty-five goes down to £81,326; leave it another five years and it is only £49,893, which means that if the pension plan is started six years later the pension is nearly halved. If the fund grows at more than 10 per cent per annum, and if you choose no return of fund, the difference is even greater.

Take no notice of colleagues who say they will start a pension plan later on when they can afford it. Not only will they never 'be able to afford it' but they have evidently not realised that what they invest in the first few years is worth all the later years' investments put together.

So, if you have a pension scheme, find out all about it. If you have none, start one today. On a final note ask yourself which combination you prefer:

£140 a week now		£130 a week now
£40 a week at retirement	or	£100 a week at retirement

Housey Housey

Little needs to be written about the advantages of owning one's own place. The difficulty for single first-time buyers is proving they have the income to raise a sufficient mortgage to buy the first place, especially when they have little to put down in cash.

One solution is to share the purchase. If it is a place which can be conveniently split up in whole or in part, then it should not affect your life-style. It will, however, certainly provide you with a much larger deposit for the next purchase, than at the first purchase.

A quick illustration will suffice. It assumes that, after tax relief, the amount spent on a house or flat being bought with a mortgage works out about the same as paying rental over a longish period of time:

1987: house purchased for £44,000 by 2 people, £4,000 saved and £40,000 borrowed from building society	1997: house is sold, after increasing in price by 10 per cent each year, for £114,125. Mortgage is paid off. Legal cost, etc., not deducted.
Cash at beginning £4,000 (£2,000 each)	Cash at end £74,125 (£37,062 each)

It is not a bad idea to make sure than you can cover any risk you undertake. The cost of covering such risks is usually small and can be coped with from part of one's income. The risk is that if one does not cover it and something serious occurs one is made bankrupt to sort it out. These are some of the items to check:

Loans. It saves everyone a lot of problems if you have sufficient insurance to enable loans to be paid off should you die; it may be that when you take out a loan you already have insurance, say on a savings plan or on your employer's pension scheme, to cover all your lending risks.

Cars. These seem to be an enormous expense with nothing back, so the risk of theft or accident should always be covered.

Health. You are *three times* as likely to become ill before retirement than to die before retirement, and if you are unable to work the effect is just as disastrous as retiring on a pittance with the added difficulty that you may not be sufficiently mobile to sort out simple tasks like shopping; and, unlike retirement, it comes as a surprise and is not anticipated.

Everything, house, car etc., is likely to go if there is no income coming in to pay for these. So 'income protection' or 'permanent health insurance', as it is sometimes called, is vital. If you had a machine in your front room which made £150 a week but was liable to go wrong occasionally, would you not pay out a few pounds a week in order to guarantee that £150 whilst it was being mended?

First, you find out how long you will be paid for if you are ill or are off work from an accident. Then you choose the kind of permanent health insurance to begin when the paid period ends. Otherwise the effect is just like that of the pensioner with no pension except the basic state one when he retires. Also, it is ideal to pay a little more and have it index-linked.

House contents and personal liability. Never mind the cost of replacing your goods if there is a fire or a flood; you can risk those if you like. What about the motorcyclist who swerves to avoid you and crashes; or the bath which overflows, damaging other flats? You may find difficulty meeting a claim for £350,000 from a brain-damaged motorcyclist or a claim from the five flats below you. House contents insurance frequently covers risks like these.

Are you a saver or a spender?
If you are the kind of person who spends anything left over at the end of the week, then pick a savings plan which has penalties for early leaving. If you are already a saver, look at what others are getting for their money. If you are receiving 5 per cent from a bank and they are making over 20 per cent on a Unit Trust investment then who is the monkey? Remember that almost everyone who took out a small savings plan some years back wishes they had taken out a bigger one.

Miscellanea
That is all except for a few general recommendations which apply to everyone, living alone or otherwise.

Making a will
Do make a will with a solicitor. Because they charge a percentage on executing wills, solicitors generally make a will for an insult rather than a fee (but ask first) and it does save a mess when you die. More important, it gives you a contact for advice for mortgage or rent problems, or even for stalling for you. For example, if a persistent salesman will not take No for an answer try referring him to your solicitor ('He okays my financial decisions') and ring the solicitor and tell him you don't want the product but find it difficult to say No.

Giving to Caesar
It is generally good to pay tax, National Insurance and VAT. Normally only crooks benefit from 'cash' deals; like

the builder who cannot be sued for a shoddy job because there is no proof he did the job. Or the nanny who retires penniless because her employers always paid her 'cash'.

The never never
The first 'never' is never to get into a debt problem you cannot cope with. The second 'never' is never to borrow against a 'wasting asset', like a car.

The secret formula is APR (Actual Percentage Rate). So if the APR on a mortgage is about 11.5 per cent *and* you receive tax relief on that, your real APR is about 8 per cent.

If you borrow for a car at '15 per cent' the APR is about 29.5 per cent which means you are paying about one-third of your loan each year in interest; rather steep, really.

Credit card companies are also to be avoided like the plague unless you have the self-discipline to pay it all off at no interest every month.

Finally, if you get into difficulty do not borrow at high interest rates to escape short-term problems; go for advice or ask your creditors for time to pay.

The man in your cupboard
Money is all about people. Find your advisers and stick to them. Send the bank manager Christmas cards and recognise your building society employees. If you are self-employed do not be afraid to ask an accountant how much he will charge. If £250 is too much for a year's accounts, tell him; and ask him for the name of a smaller-time accountant than he. Go back to that helpful house-contents insurance man for a quote on the endowment rather than be pushed by the estate agent, who will never help out on any other problem, into going with him.

Remember that people are usually 'interested' in giving financial advice; the building society has a target of endowments to achieve, the accountant gets a kick back on pensions sold through his 'independent advisers', and the bank manager wants you to get the bank to be your executor. Even *Which* magazine has a bias against organisations which make profits, and recommend 'mutual' ones (*Which* is non-profit-making), even if their clients do not get the best deal.

Keeping accounts

Any book-keeping: keep it simple, and keep up to date, especially with the taxman, who will be incredibly helpful if you try to help him.

It may seem odd that a chapter addressed to those with 'almost no money' should have so much advice on how to spend it and so much discouragement to borrowers (except those borrowing at a good rate against an appreciating asset).

Look again, however, and it is clear that two threads run through the chapter. One is that the risk of not spending a little now is that one may become a burden to others or a bankrupt later on. The second is that everything suggested is only a small part of expenditure to which one is already committed.

For example, if you go for a job interview you expect to be paid enough to fund a reasonable pension: if not, turn down the job. If you buy and maintain a house or car the extra cost of proper insurance is insignificant: so if you cannot afford the extras maybe you should not have made the purchase in the first place.

Funny money

Have some fun – take a little bit of a risk occasionally (e.g. with share applications from big companies or overseas funds of large UK insurance companies).

For further information

Radio

'Moneybox' BBC Radio 4

Newspapers

Daily Mail (MoneyMail)	Wednesday
Financial Times	Saturday
The Times	Saturday
Daily Telegraph	Saturday

Books

Burr, Rosemary, *100 Money Saving Ideas*. Rosters 1985, £2.00.

Consumers Association, *What Will My Pension Be*? 1985, £5.95 (excludes Government proposals Dec. 1985 and 1986 legislation).

Moffit, Douglas, *The Family Money Book*. Dent Paperbacks, 1986, £3.95.

Tait, Nikki, *Investors Chronicle Beginners Guide to the Stock-Market*. Penguin Books, 1986, £3.95.

Guardian Money Guide. Willow Books, 1986, £4.95.

Periodicals

Which? Quarterly (incorporates money reports formerly published separately in *Money Which*)

Money Management Monthly

Planned Savings Monthly

Which? is for everyone. The other two are useful for comparing companies on different products and should be on the desk (along with the *Financial Times*) of any competent investment or pensions adviser.

Free booklets

The Stock Exchange, Throgmorton Street, London EC3.

Company Pensions Information Centre, 7 Old Park Lane, London W17 3LJ.

Most big banks, insurance companies and Post Offices have booklets of general interest giving practical advice.

Free advice

Central Office of Information, Hercules Road, London SE1 (01–928–2345).

Department of Health and Social Security (local offices).

Notes

1. Civil servant readers who are convinced that their maximum is 40/80 will be puzzled about the reference to two-thirds final salary. Equally, multinationals' employees will be puzzled to hear that they are no better off than civil servants. In fact, the calculation above is a gross simplification which closely approximates to reality. Thus a civil servant who wisely invested the 135/40 tax-free sum and who then enjoyed the state pension (less the deduction of about £67 per annum) would have the equivalent of a two-thirds index-linked pension – possibly better. The employee of a large City solicitor partnership or of a multinational would probably expect two-thirds increasing annually plus a tax free sum, plus other benefits.
2. In fact there is no fund; the Government simply takes all employees' contributions for the Exchequer and then takes pensions from the same place.

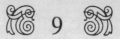 9

A maiden all forlorn – why should you be?

There have been times when pagan religions sacrificed young virgin girls to their gods.

The modern pagan world is still doing it, and it is a terribly sad thing to witness. I worked some time ago with a young woman who was living with her boyfriend. She, in conversation one day, spoke of the time when she had first started taking the contraceptive pill. She was an amusing and intelligent speaker and she had been about seventeen at the time in question. 'Cor,' she said, 'you should have seen what they gave me. They said I wouldn't be safe for a month so they gave me a supply of condoms. My life! They gave me enough for twice a night and I didn't even enjoy sex.'

In that last sentence is summed up the whole sad state of affairs (no pun intended) which exists today. And it *is* sad. Society had taught her that she ought to indulge in sex whether she liked it or not (or was truly ready for it or not). Society had also taught her boyfriend of the time that it was reasonable to expect sexual gratification from her. We all know someone like this woman. It may even have applied to you at one time. The result of this thinking (or lack of thinking) is that young people are understandably embarrassed to admit to an incredulous world that they are not sleeping with their current boyfriend/girlfriend. Well I've got news for anybody in this situation. You don't have to tell. It's nobody's business but yours.

Sex is a big bugbear to many people. It's the thing Christians are most often accused of having a guilt complex about. Personally I think that's as clear a case of transference as any other. However, this is not a book about the sexual hang-ups of the non-Christian.

Sex, as we all know, is one of God's most precious gifts to us. It is clearly meant by design and intent to be a particularly enriching and beautiful experience (which is why we all want to do it, of course).

The Bible doesn't have an awful lot to say on the subject of sex. I like to think that one of the main conclusions we can draw from this is not a reticence on God's part (of course not). But rather that if our eyes are on the Lord and our feet set in his path then our attitudes to sex, as with every other aspect of life, will fall naturally and healthily into place. For the Christian the famous exhortation from the book of Proverbs, 'Who can find a virtuous woman? for her price is above rubies' (Proverbs 31.10), is as sound today as it ever was. The modern virtuous woman (or man for that matter) is often made out by God's enemies to be something of a twit, and we all know the joke that is made out of the last part of that line, '. . . her price is above Ruby's'. Ha! ha! Very funny, but not very subtle.

Joking apart, it is a sad reflection that in the eyes of the secular society in which we live a virtuous woman has simply degenerated into a 'sensible' one. One, that is, who will go on the pill or in some other way be 'fitted out' before she starts sleeping with her boyfriend. This often happens at an astonishingly young age, but we all know what it's like to be young and think that we own the world and know all there is to know. Sadly, it could be several years and quite some lovers later before they discover they really were too young to embark on their sexual careers. The point is that we are not asked to abstain from extra-marital sex in order to deprive us of something. All through the Old Testament, and more especially in the New, God's message to us is underlined by the fact (and act) of his giving. He gives us the whole of creation. He gave us our very lives and of course he gives us *his* very life in his Holy Spirit and his Son.

God is totally giving. We even have his word on that. 'I come that they might have life in abundance.' So if we actually think that we are being deprived of something we must take a good honest look at our attitudes and resolutely take them to our Heavenly Father.

Are we deprived?

No of course we're not. We know that because we have been told so by our minister or counsellor or in Christian books. That is, we know it intellectually. But do we know it inside ourselves, out of our own experience with God? Well, we're all at different stages in our pilgrimage through this world, so some will be more aware than others of how the Lord can fill that seemingly bottomless pit of aching and wanting and turn our sorrow into joy. Even if the Lord keeps you single, there is no need to become the archetypal dried-up old spinster; in fact, there's every reason why you shouldn't. Life is indeed rich and can be full. The day-to-day walk with God of the single person can yield the same ripe fruit for the Kingdom that the married can offer. We are called to be witnesses whatever our circumstances in life, and in offering these circumstances to God we are all working with each other as one in the Mystical Body of Christ.

Of course we are all open to attack from Satan, and there will be times when it is difficult not to get depressed or even bitter about one's solo status. If you are a prayerful person and your relationship with God is an open and growing one, if you are active in your church and other spheres of work and social life, and if you have good sound friends with whom you can share confidences, then you won't need me to tell you how to get through those times. You, along with every other Christian, have a perfect opportunity in the midst of your sufferings to discover that God is indeed faithful. If you accept your cross, preferably gladly, but at least with resignation, you will find that joy really does come in the morning (figuratively speaking). You can offer to God your bitterness, frustration, depression or whatever negative quality you are feeling. Millions before you have done it, and certainly millions after you will also learn that he really does take up the burden you have cast on him. And in the joy that comes with this wonderful lightening of your load you begin to see that there was a point to your suffering in the first place. That your relationship with the Lord has gone a step further. What Satan would convince you was punishment, has yielded an awareness of privilege. In fact, you've grown. God didn't bring you the hour of suffering; he certainly didn't wish it on you. Satan, you will come to realise, was trying to gain foothold in his campaign to lead you to your death. But Jesus, as he proved in the Gospels, has conquered death, and so he conquers it in us in these smaller steps through our lives when we rise to be joyful again. A dim reflection of the great resurrection to which we all look forward.

You may often feel, in times of misery, that your sorrow stems solely from the fact that you are single. I'm sure that for married people the reverse is the case. When they are going through a term of trial it seems that all their problems arise from being married. The truth is that Satan isn't particular whether we're married or single. He will use whatever situation we are in and try to make us feel utterly miserable about it. 'If only I could have a nice, loving, sexual relationship with someone,' might be a typical single person's cry. 'It's all sex, sex, sex; it really gets me down,' is the sort of thing that might be expected from an equally disgruntled married person. If we're sensible we realise that the other person's grass is never really greener.

Of course, the world we're living in is not much help.

I think that another reason why there isn't much said about sex in the Bible is that in biblical times it didn't have to be said. Chastity concerning pre-marital sex was built into the general mores of society. And of course this was true even of our own society until quite recently. Lots of us can still remember a time when 'nice girls didn't'. Well, society has changed, as you know, and its mores are vastly different. Sex is pushed at us from every angle. It will be in much of the conversation of your non-Christian friends and almost certainly in the expectation of your average, carnal non-Christian man. It is used to sell everything from soap to cigarettes. Sex and sexual delight are promoted in every town, city and village in the country. It's in the newspapers (I'll spare you all the jokes about page-three girls), on the television and in virtually every art form there is. Whole industries are getting rich on sex. And the spirit of human-kind is the poorer because of it.

Because of this you may well find that you've looked at the business of chastity from every angle known and a few that aren't. Perhaps you've even studied this question in the hope of finding a loophole.

The truth is that there isn't one. The biblical position is clear. Our bodies, as Saint Paul tells us, are temples of the Holy Spirit. 'But he who is united to the Lord becomes one spirit with him. Shun immorality. Every other sin which a man commits is outside the body; but the immoral man sins against his own body. Do you not know that your body is a temple of the Holy Spirit within you, which you have from God? You are not your own. You were bought with a price. So glorify God in your body' (1 Corinthians 6.17–20). And even though references to sex in the Bible are scarce, each one that does appear follows the same line of guiding us in the practice of continence and self-control.

Nobody says it is easy.

It's especially not easy when we're talking about mastur-bation. This has to be looked at in the same light as pre-marital sex. It's a harder temptation to resist, of course, because at least in the case of intercourse you have to have access to a consenting adult. But masturbation can be indulged in all on your lonesome (and it's because you are on your lonesome that you may want to do it).

It's awfully bad for your eyes

Yes, well they used to say that didn't they? (the all knowing 'them'). There's absolutely no medical evidence backing up such a claim, of course, but actually speaking I think there's a certain sub-conscious folk-wisdom in it. Naturally I don't mean in the literal sense. But we often use the analogy of sight when we are talking about understanding. 'Oh I see what you mean,' we say after somebody has been getting blue in the face trying to hammer home some point to us. 'Yes I see it now,' we continue as they breathe huge sighs of relief at overcoming our obtuseness. So we use the term sight to indicate understanding, perception. And as a result of masturbation our perception of sex as part of a shared, loving relationship can become rather dulled. Sex is meant to be a giving as well as a receiving experience. Masturbation is totally self-satisfying. Sex is meant to be outgoing. Masturbation is totally inward turning. We have no partner to try to please, we only have our own timing to think about and only our own satisfaction to work for.

The act of masturbation, unlike sexual intercourse with a marriage partner, cannot be offered up to the praise of the Lord. And here is a clue to the fact that really we know it's wrong; it's something people try to hide. It's not done in the daylight usually, it's in the dark and it's something glossed over in the examination of our consciences. It's also dangerously habit-forming. Basically, the temptation always seems to be strongest once you're in bed; and though you might have heard all the good advice for countering it such as getting up again and reading a book or some such other innocent activity until you either feel sleepy or the inclination has passed, dealing with this problem is entirely personal and only you can know what works for you. My own feeling is that, temptation or no temptation, once you're in bed at night you ideally wish to stay there until morning and resent even having to get up for a trip to the loo. I'm sure a lot of people choose to lie there and suffer.

Just remember that you can offer the temptation to the Lord and ask him to deal with it, and in this way, once again, your trials and tribulations will be turned to good account. As I've already said, nobody says it's easy.

Actually, if sex can be habit-forming, so can chastity. It does get easier. There's no trick involved. No matter which way you turn on this issue, if you are truly seeking God's will, whatever path you try to explore you will meet him at some point along it, very lovingly and gently (and forgivingly), showing you that there's only one way of Life. But also, that the benefits of following that way are vast and infinitely more rewarding than an illicit, guilt-ridden and, quite likely, unsatisfactory sexual experience. It takes prayer, it takes a lively growing faith and a full, active itinerary to keep strong on the issue of chastity. But it does get easier. Temptation isn't a permanent house-guest (let's face it, how often do you meet a man you go weak at the knees for?). Most people are only truly attacked now and again. Among the ongoing, everyday problems of living out the Christian life, sexual temptation, most of the time, is not one of the major irritants. You'll find it a lot harder being nice and patient with the completely impossible woman in your office than resisting the attentions of the man from the accounts department or keeping your hands under control when you're in bed. Be of good cheer. God will hold you up every step of the way. But you must take the problem to him. He likes to be asked.

But what if . . .?
Well yes, in a moment of weakness it can and does happen now and again. What if you've fallen into temptation, be it masturbation, sexual intercourse or even lusting after someone in your heart. Well okay, what if you have? The first thing you have to seek is to be at peace with God. If your church maintains the sacrament of confession you will naturally go along, and you probably already know that you can't tell a priest anything he hasn't heard before. If you

belong to one of the other church traditions, then you will repent in a manner according to the teachings of that church. It's not for me to tell you how to go about any of this.

But the main thing is, having made your peace with God, you must forget your fall. Because he most assuredly has. Put it behind you. You do not have to discuss this with anyone. As with your non-Christian colleagues on the question of abstinence, the same rule applies. It's nobody's business but yours. The best advice you can have here is that given by the Lord himself to the woman taken in adultery, 'Go thy way and sin no more.'

If you find that, after repentance, your sin still weighs on you, you may need to seek the advice and counsel of someone at your church. Your minister will be only too willing to set your mind at rest.

Oh, but it's too embarrassing, I couldn't talk to anyone
Well, yes, it might be embarrassing. What you might feel you need is to speak to someone in a totally anonymous fashion. There are only two ways I know of doing this. One is to write to the problem page of a magazine. The Christian papers and magazines give very sound, Gospel-based advice and will respect your anonymity.

The other way is by talking it over with a priest or minister from a church other than the one you attend. It doesn't even have to be the same denomination as yours. The ministers of all the churches are only too pleased if they can comfort a soul in distress and they won't worry if you are not one of their regular flock.

However you seek help, if you have this kind of problem just remember, whoever you go to, your counsellor has already been through all these temptations and may have even fallen into them just as you have.

So now it's all over and you're getting on with the business of living. But what if it's not all over? What if the consequences have only just begun?

What if you're pregnant?

It's going to be a shock. It may well seem like a disaster. You may be completely knocked out, devastated and terrified. You may feel that your life is over. Well, in fact, a new life has begun for someone, and God is using you to bring it into the world. It's important here, especially in the face of any prejudice you might encounter, to remember that, at the very best, human beings can only make love. God makes babies. Modern thinking and genetic engineering constantly try to make us think differently, but there is no getting away from the truth of the matter that sexual intercourse is inextricably linked to procreation. And creation is the business of God. We on earth can only ever hope to be his assistants in this. So, though you may be ashamed of the sin you committed, there is never any reason to be ashamed of the baby that has resulted. Unfortunately, any privacy you wanted to maintain about your activities has now gone out of the window.

Some churches are more rigid in their attitudes to children born out of wedlock than others, and only you know how your particular congregation might react. Even here, though, once people's initial shock has worn off, you could find yourself pleasantly surprised to be given support and comfort from unexpected quarters. But, whatever church you belong to, you ought to be able to expect solid, non-judgemental help that is spiritual, emotional and practical; and if you are given the cold shoulder and looked down on by anyone because of your condition it is to their shame and not yours. You've repented of *your* sin and you have every right to look to your fellow Christians for succour. If the resources of your church are limited and your family unable or unwilling (or just too far away), there are several ports of call, in addition to the Social Services. Don't worry; from these and from within the Christian family you can receive all the help you need. From the pregnancy test onwards you can get practical, emotional and spiritual support. You can be guided through the whole business of maternity benefits and social security. If necessary you can be helped with accommodation and even baby clothes. If you choose adoption, they will take on the burden of all those details for you. It really isn't the end of the world.

You may, for instance, have exams coming up or just be starting a new job. Well, pregnancy isn't a disease. Pregnant women don't lose the ability to read and write when they conceive. There may be any number of things in your life which it appears your baby will either interfere with or put paid to altogether. In fact, you may be tempted to think about an abortion. Please don't. 'Thou shalt not kill,' applies here equally to your child as to a full-grown person. And the baby is also your neighbour to be loved as yourself. Life begins at conception, and your baby is not a potential human being but a human being with potential. Apart from that, though, there is increasing evidence that abortion can be damaging, not only emotionally, but physically as well (it can even cause future sterility).

Most of the things you were doing in your life can be carried on with, even though you are now pregnant. Even if they have to be postponed, nine months is not such a very long time (and it won't even be that by the time the pregnancy is confirmed). If there is any plan that has to be ditched altogether or drastically changed, be sure the Lord will lead you to realise that your baby is more important.

One thing I would strongly advise is that you should on no account go for help to some of the 'pregnancy advice' agencies which you might see advertised in the press or on posters. Some of them seem to operate as little more than abortion agencies, and the only exception I know that advertises in a secular way is 'Life' which is an excellent organisation and I can heartily recommend them. You need have no fears either for yourself or your baby if you approach them.

It may be that you'll get help and support from the father of the child. There might even be talk of marriage, either from him himself, or in the form of pressure from your church – especially if he is also a Christian. An important 'don't' here is . . . just don't. There is only one reason for getting married to anyone. For the Christian, you must be convinced, regardless of your pregnancy, that this is the man God wants you to marry. It's no good trying to make yourself believe you're in love if you know in your heart of hearts that you're not. And it's even worse to compound your sin (which no longer burdens you anyway) with the even worse one of entering any alliance other than the one to which God is leading you. In short, pregnancy is not a good enough reason in itself to get married. If you were already planning to marry, then of course you have no problem; but marriage is truly '. . . a holy state, not to be entered lightly . . .' And if any pressure to marry is coming at you from your fellow Christians, then quite frankly they should know better. There is more help given to single parents today than at any other time in the past and, you never know, in the future God may bring you to the man he has chosen for you.

Salacious . . . erot . . . dirty pict . . . pornography

I suppose it doesn't matter what you call it, does it? It's been around for centuries of course. (I'm no historian but I have done the tourist stint through the ruins of Pompei.) It's a curious thing all the same. For instance, I'm an avid reader. If I'm not sleeping or eating the chances are that I've got my nose stuck in a book. My favourite type of novels are murder mysteries and spy thrillers. Whenever I've finished such a book I put it aside feeling satisfied with having had a good read. What I don't feel like doing is going out and murdering someone or breaking into the Russian embassy to steal top secret documents.

Pornography isn't like that. It doesn't leave you feeling satisfied. It leaves you feeling (a) most definitely unsatisfied, and (b) that a good read is the least of your problems. You will, in fact, want to go and do exactly what you have just been reading about, or looking at pictures of, or watching. Whether it's in the form of films, magazines or extremely graphic literature, pornography is something to be avoided. It will definitely make you frustrated and could lead you into sin. It can even lead to crime. Not long ago in a court case concerning sexual abuse, the defendant actually admitted that it was after reading pornography that he went out and committed the crimes for which he was on trial.

There are those who will say that some of it reaches the level of art, and they call it erotica. That may be so, but the question here is not how artistically a couple might be making love – sorry, copulating – for the benefit of the camera, but the effect it is having on you. That effect is likely to be upsetting and you'll only feel sorry and degraded later when you've calmed down again. Looking at or reading pornographic material can be a bit like letting someone else do your masturbating for you. And that's without the fact that it can cause you to end up indulging in that very activity. The best advice here is to avoid it as an occasion of sin. This might be easier said than done, especially when, say, at work a magazine is being handed round and you fear that, as the only person not looking at it, you will seem like a prude. You can pass up the magazine (or the invitation to a blue film or a strip show) without appearing prudish. A very calm, unruffled 'Thanks all the same but that's not how I get my kicks,' goes over a lot better than, 'Yeuk! it's filthy and disgusting and I'm not interested.' Which is probably a lie anyway because you wouldn't be normal if you weren't interested. We're meant to be interested. We're sexual human beings after all.

But I'm attracted to my own sex

If, as we have discovered through the Bible and in observing the general created order of things, the place of sexual intercourse is between a man and a woman in the comfort, security and sacredness of the marriage partnership, we have to conclude that any acts not complying with these conditions must be wrong. In the cases of homosexuality or any other deviation, everything that's already been said about masturbation applies here.

I'm not trying to decry any feelings you have which may be very real and very deep, and it might seem strange to you that you are being told not to put them into practice. The thing is, our desires and feelings alone are not enough of a guide in deciding what our actions ought to be. The whole question must be looked at in terms of what those actions do to those involved (as well as you) and where they are leading. (Clearly, intercourse between a man and a woman is the only sexual act that can lead anywhere.)

If you seek the help of a counsellor, don't worry about what he/she might think of you. They've heard it all before. They won't be shocked by anything you tell them and they won't think you're disgusting; even if *you* do.

One other thing though. Whatever else you do, don't let your sexual proclivities keep you from coming to church and taking a full part in the various activities.

Be involved in your congregation, build up good, sound relationships with other members of the church and confess Jesus as your Lord. You are loved by him the same as all your brothers and sisters and don't let your sexual inclinations cause you to think otherwise (Satan will try anything, remember). Remember above all that your situation is not insoluble. It is not for nothing that Jesus is also called the Great Healer.

Your counsellor

Just a final note on the subject of counsellors.

They can be of enormous help and support to you through

a difficult time, whether your problem be emotional, sexual, spiritual or whatever.

But it is as well to be aware that sometimes more harm than good can be done by well-meaning people who aren't really competent to deal with your problem. Furthermore, even if your counsellor is a fully trained person he/she may not be a Christian and needless confusion can arise from the possible undermining of your faith. That's not to say that you should *only* seek a Christian counsellor but you should certainly have one who is sympathetic to your faith. Floyd McClung's book, *The Father Heart of God* (Kingsway Publications) has, in its appendix, a list of things you would be wise to ask your prospective counsellor, and it is with the publisher's permission that I reproduce them here.

1. The best way to select a counsellor or psychiatrist is to rely on a referral from a respected church leader, family doctor or friend who has had previous contact with the professional and knows them and their work personally.

2. A competent professional is not threatened if a prospective patient calls and tactfully asks about their qualifications, their theoretical orientation, and the type of licence they hold.

3. Fees should be discussed before any commitment is made to treatment. A therapist should be willing to give at least a rough estimation as to how many sessions are going to be necessary, and at what intervals they will need to occur.

4. It is a good idea to find out how much experience the therapist has had in dealing with your particular problem. Some therapists are obviously better suited to certain areas.

5. Find out how much of the therapist's counselling is based on God's word. Does his/her counselling differ from that of a secular counsellor?

Epilogue

So that's it, really; if not in a nutshell, at least between the covers of this book.

I haven't written a personal testimony, but having read this far you will have already realised that I've drawn here and there on my own experiences and those of my friends and acquaintances. Nor is this book meant to be, 'The Complete Guide to . . .' You may have ways of doing things, or ideas about living alone, that I haven't mentioned (or thought of only on the day the manuscript went to press!) So, though I hope this book will be of help to you, I also hope that its usefulness will be more in the capacity of a springboard rather than a workshop manual. After all, it's only supposed to be a guide to a way of living, not a plan of campaign.

Your time of living alone may last a few months, a few years or for the rest of your life. But, however long it lasts for you, I hope that through it you can deepen your relationship with God and with those around you, and that you can discover and deepen your knowledge of yourself. You have been presented with a great opportunity to develop in all three of these vital areas. Jesus Christ came that we might have life in abundance. That's what he wants for me and for you; that's you stuck in your tiny bedsit in the middle of a bustling great city, and you in that isolated farmhouse miles from anywhere. It's all there waiting for you, everything you need in full measure. Living alone does not mean living on the fringes of a mainly married society or looking in from the outside at other people's families.

You're already a partner in the most important marriage of all, and a member of the biggest family you're ever going to know. You have no need to explain yourself to anybody. You haven't failed in any way and you are not inadequate. It's only going to seem like solitary confinement if you let it, and you don't have to let it. You're you, you're beloved and you have a path to follow which is completely unique to you. I still stand by what I said at the beginning of chapter 3. Living alone can be tremendous fun. I certainly enjoy it and I hope you will too.